LITTLE BANQUETS FOR ORDINARY PEOPLE

LITTLE BANQUETS FOR ORDINARY PEOPLE

Epiphanies of Every Day

Edward J. Farrell

ALBA·HOUSE NEW·YORK

SOCIETY OF ST. PAUL, 2187 VICTORY BLVD., STATEN ISLAND, NEW YORK 10314

ST PAULS

Library of Congress Cataloging-in-Publication Data

Farrell, Edward J.
Little banquets for ordinary people: epiphanies of every day / Edward J. Farrell.
p. cm.
ISBN 0-8189-0873-4
1. Spiritual life—Catholic Church—Meditations. I. Title.

BX2182.2 .F375 2000
242—dc21

99-055135

Produced and designed in the United States of America by the Fathers and Brothers of the Society of St. Paul, 2187 Victory Boulevard, Staten Island, New York 10314-6603, as part of their communications apostolate.

ISBN: 0-8189-0873-4

Printing Information:

Current Printing - first digit	1	2	3	4	5	6	7	8	9	10

Year of Current Printing - first year shown

2000	2001	2002	2003	2004	2005	2006	2007	2008	2009

Dedication

To Vincent Abate (1930-1991), my brother-in-law, beau-frère — a beautiful man — a teamster union president with honesty, integrity, and devotion of the poor man of Assisi.

With gratitude to Lynn Salata for her transcribing, manuscript work, and energetic tenacity in the writing of this book.

For the people of St. Daniel Parish, Clarkston, Michigan, who welcomed me so deeply into their hearts and faith that together we "hatched" these "little banquets."

TABLE OF CONTENTS

Celebrate Yourself!

The Epiphany Banquet

PREFACE

"Every question possesses a power that does not lie in any answer." — *Elie Wiesel*

"…and He said to them, 'Why are you talking about having no bread? Do you still not understand, still not realize? Are your minds closed? Have you eyes and do not see, ears and do not hear? or do you not remember?' Then He said to them, 'Do you still not realize?'" (Mk 8:17-21)

Mt 17:10	*The disciples put this question to Him…*
Mt 21:24	*I too will ask you a question…*
Mk 8:27	*On the way, He asked his disciples this question…*
Mk 9:11	*Finally they put to him this question…*
Mk 13:3	*John and Andrew began to question Him privately…*
Lk 7:20	*The Baptizer sends us to you with this question…*
Jn 18:7	*Jesus put the question to them again…*
Jn 21:13	*He answered with a question…*
Jn 21:16	*A second time He put His question…*
Jn 21:20	*They wanted to question Him more carefully…*

"As for Mary, she treasured all these things and continually pondered them in her heart." (Lk 2:19)

And 12 years later, "His mother stored up all these things in her heart." (Lk 2:52)

> Jesus' first words in the Gospels of Luke and John come as a question, "Why were you looking for me?" (Lk 2:49) and "What do you want?" (Jn 1:38)
>
> "Jesus Christ is the Incarnate Question and Answer of God about the true goodness and direction of our lives. Even the shortest Gospel, Mark, reflects the tension of the Question that Jesus is for all human life with its no less than 118 questions of which more than half are raised by Jesus Himself."
>
> — *John Navone*

Gathered here are reflections, "little banquets," for ordinary people, for people whose names the world does not know. What questions does Jesus ask in our day? Raised here is a banquet of questions. Questions to draw us deeper into ourselves. Questions to enrich our relationship with God — Father, Son, and Holy Spirit. Questions inviting us to enter Scripture. Questions awakening us to kinship with one other. We are guided by our questions and reflection. Through them, this work becomes yours — intimate, exclusive, personal. Each one coming to a banquet will choose and savor in their unique way. In this sense, each will have read a different book, for much of what you "read" will come from within yourself.

"Epiphany" is one of the favorite words of the great Irish writer, James Joyce. In the most ordinary and least of things, he intuited that there is an immense energy, light, power, and beauty waiting to burst through. If one but took the time to look, to contemplate, to ponder and treasure these moments in one's heart. In so doing, one becomes an Epiphany, celebrating the almost unbearable lightness of Faith.

How deeply Jesus knows our hunger, our weariness! Are there any more comforting words than His invitation, "Come to me all you who are weary and tired and *I will refresh you*"? The Word of God is comfort, therapy, healing, energy. His Word is sacramental — rendering His loving Presence to me and enabling me to be lovingly present to myself.

My horizon is always shrinking, but He draws me into His heart and expands me to the dimensions of His love. The Word that He sowed in me when I was a child, He keeps watering and cultivating until its roots sink deeper and deeper in me and begin to bear fruit in me, in my life. The Word is one that I am not ready to hear, that I resist. And yet, my very resistance embeds it more and more in me. The Words have been waiting in my inner storage place waiting for the moment and occasion for their light to illuminate the darkness and fear.

The cumulative deposit of the Word, heard or read, year after year, wraps me round and round like the yearly ring of a tree. The gentle, caressing Word, the Word shot like an arrow piercing my evasion, catching me as I run from Him, follows me with "unperturbèd pace, majestic instancy." The Word lingering in my unconsciousness waits to spring up and Easter in me. How long does it take for the Word to penetrate all the levels in me until it transplants my heart! How long does it take to move from my heart and head into my hands and feet!

God's Word has never stopped echoing. The Word does not end. The Word is always new, always fresh. As a priest of 40 years, I continue to be astonished recognizing that God's Word is a perennial flower. Year after year it breaks through the hard earth, the thorns, and the brambles. And it blossoms forth.

Every year is special, but the biblical years are even more special, more symbol. As I live my 41st year of ordination, I am compelled to contemplate the paralytic who was waiting for 38 years. His soul-filled cry, "I have no one," and my cry, "I have Someone," — One who is always with me, always speaking, whispering to me. Each of God's Words is full of life, full of creative power. His Words identify me, call me, empower me, send me forth!

Each Word is like a pilot light, always gently burning — softly, yet, at any unsuspecting moment, capable of releasing immense heat and energy. The Word of God is always smoldering in some hidden place deep within.

In the midst of the daily bad and sad news of the media, how good it is to pick up the Good News and to see and hear what God has to speak to my heart today.

> "If today you hear His voice in the desert, harden not your hearts." (Ps 95)
>
> "Let your face shed its light upon us." (Ps 64)
>
> "Sing a new song to the Lord."
>
> "O! to dwell in the house of the Lord all the days of my life."
>
> "O! to be drawn into the prayer of the Lord each day of my life."
>
> "We do not know how to pray." (Rm 8)

We do not know our hidden prayer, the prayer that never finds its way into words. We are like musical instruments; they do not produce music of themselves. In the hands of the great musician, from her touch, his breath, a new song, a new symphony rises to the heavens and spreads throughout the universe! We recognize our spirit and our heart when God puts words to our inner melody through His psalms and Word.

Biblical Abbreviations

OLD TESTAMENT

Genesis	Gn	Nehemiah	Ne	Baruch	Ba
Exodus	Ex	Tobit	Tb	Ezekiel	Ezk
Leviticus	Lv	Judith	Jdt	Daniel	Dn
Numbers	Nb	Esther	Est	Hosea	Ho
Deuteronomy	Dt	1 Maccabees	1 M	Joel	Jl
Joshua	Jos	2 Maccabees	2 M	Amos	Am
Judges	Jg	Job	Jb	Obadiah	Ob
Ruth	Rt	Psalms	Ps	Jonah	Jon
1 Samuel	1 S	Proverbs	Pr	Micah	Mi
2 Samuel	2 S	Ecclesiastes	Ec	Nahum	Na
1 Kings	1 K	Song of Songs	Sg	Habakkuk	Hab
2 Kings	2 K	Wisdom	Ws	Zephaniah	Zp
1 Chronicles	1 Ch	Sirach	Si	Haggai	Hg
2 Chronicles	2 Ch	Isaiah	Is	Malachi	Ml
Ezra	Ezr	Jeremiah	Jr	Zechariah	Zc
		Lamentations	Lm		

NEW TESTAMENT

Matthew	Mt	Ephesians	Eph	Hebrews	Heb
Mark	Mk	Philippians	Ph	James	Jm
Luke	Lk	Colossians	Col	1 Peter	1 P
John	Jn	1 Thessalonians	1 Th	2 Peter	2 P
Acts	Ac	2 Thessalonians	2 Th	1 John	1 Jn
Romans	Rm	1 Timothy	1 Tm	2 John	2 Jn
1 Corinthians	1 Cor	2 Timothy	2 Tm	3 John	3 Jn
2 Corinthians	2 Cor	Titus	Tt	Jude	Jude
Galatians	Gal	Philemon	Phm	Revelation	Rv

You Are Invited!

COME TO THE BANQUET, NOW

Who is this God who lavishes gifts upon us? Gifts too numerous to comprehend. How extravagant is God's gift of changing seasons: the movement from spring to summer to autumn to winter to spring! An endless cycle of change in all God's creation! There is more to seasons than the passage of time. We also live "seasons" in our lives. We are all a little older than we were last year. Our eyesight, our hearing, our bodies are not as they were before. We are changing. We are growing. We are moving. We are going someplace. Where will we arrive? What is the direction, the trajectory of our life? What lies ahead of us? What will it be to have spent all our days? And what will it be like in the Kingdom to come?

It is good for us to stretch our minds and our hearts to wonder what it is all about. How do you image the Kingdom of Heaven? Sometimes you've seen writings on walls or highway viaducts: "Where will you spend eternity?" It is good to think and to wonder where we will wind up. Some people carry in their minds an image of a courtroom, that place of final judgment where we will be judged in terms of the way we lived our lives. That's one image. We have a much different image in Jesus' parable of the wedding banquet.

Jesus so often speaks in parables. Parables are stories that are intended to involve you, to invite your mind and heart to explore: What is He talking about? How am I involved? Where am I in the story? How do you see yourself at the wedding banquet, the banquet of the parable? *You are invited.* Have you heard the invitation. What will it be like?

What was the most memorable banquet you've ever attended? Perhaps you've seen on television the coronation of the Queen of England, or the wedding of Charles and Diana. Imagine the banquets held for those occasions. A long, long time ago now, on October 13, 1953, I was invited to meet the Holy Father with Cardinal Mooney. There were just five or six of us together. I was but a young lad at the time. What a moment it was! On the following day, the 14th, there was the dedication of the North American College in Rome. The Holy Father attended the dedication. All the diplomatic corps of Rome was there. I was standing in line as the Holy Father passed by. I could have reached out and touched Pius XII and our ambassador, Clare Booth Luce. It was magnificent. I felt as though I was in a different world — and the banquet afterward was something I have never forgotten.

Do you have a favorite experience of a banquet? How do you see yourself being invited to the banquet of the Lord? "God will prepare a whole mountain filled with the finest food and wine." What a banquet we will have when we come into the Kingdom! Day by day we are invited to recognize that there is something unimaginably wonderful ahead of us. We are called to anticipate what God is preparing for us. Jesus tells us, "I am going ahead of you to prepare a place for you and when it is ready I will come for you."

The parable of the wedding banquet is a strange one: the king sent out the invitations, but those who received the invitations ignored them. (Imagine ignoring the invitation to the president's inaugural ball, or the governor's dinner.) Perhaps everyone ignored the invitation because they were so busy; like us they had too many things to do. The king sent his servants out to the highways and byways commanding, "Compel them to come in. I want my banquet to be filled."

Not many are called, but fewer allow themselves to be chosen. You are called. You respond and come to a banquet: the tiny, little, wee banquet of the Eucharist. Do you come prepared? We prepare ourselves for that most blessed banquet by our faithfulness, coming week after week to the little banquet of the Lord to receive His Body and Blood. And by receiving His Body and Blood, we are united, we are in communion.

The mystics speak of a "spousal union." Imagine what that would be like, to be one in God: Father, Son, and Holy Spirit. That is our destiny. In that communion we will come to know ourselves as we've never known ourselves in this life. We will see Him. We will experience Him. We will be in Him. And for the first time we will know who we truly are and what it is all about. What a magnificent reality lies ahead! Think about it. Let it resonate in your heart. It is out of this that our peace, our joy, and our union with Him unfolds day by day.

You are invited. The banquet is ready. The little banquet of His Body and Blood, in some way, is a mystical experience, a spousal union. We are never to be alone. Here is "the Way, the Truth, and the Life." Every step you take, every breath you breathe, you are not alone. He is with you. He is preparing you, creating in you a taste and a longing for what lies ahead. But He is with you every step of the way.

You are invited. You are invited to dream dreams, to see visions, to know that He has come to you, to know He walks with you, talks with you, and tells you who you are and who you are to become. The banquet is right here. *You are invited.* Ask Jesus to help you expand your mind and heart to recognize the gift you receive: the mystical union that the Eucharist is.

I'M GOING TO MEET THE KING!

When you think of Jesus, what's your favorite title? What's your name for Him? How do you experience Him? What do you get excited about in regard to Jesus? Today, we still use the word, "king," and yet it's not a word that excites most people. We celebrate Jesus as Shepherd. Certainly that's one of our favorite titles of Jesus: that He is our Shepherd. He is our healer. He is our companion. The one who's always with us. He's the one who forgives, the one who understands. The Way, the Truth, and the Life. He is the Light of the world. We have so many different titles of Jesus. The word, "king," is probably the last in our litany of expressing who Jesus is. But He is our King. Not like the kings of world history, not even like King David and King Arthur, Richard the Lion Hearted, even St. Louis, King of France. Jesus is not a king of power. Jesus is a hidden king. The only time He wore a crown was the day of His death, a crown of thorns. The only time He wore royal robes was when the soldiers mocked Him and placed a purple cloak upon Him. But when He was questioned, "Are you a king?", He said, "Yes, but my kingdom is not of this world." The only throne He had was the throne of the cross. Over Him were written the letters, "I.N.R.I.," "Jesu Nazarenus Rex Judaeorum." Jesus of Nazareth, King of the Jews.

Each of us is a member of a kingdom. Did you ever notice the phrase: "...a kingdom prepared for you from the foundation of the world"? Jesus is a king. There is something of His kingdom in each one of us. We have a capacity to admire. Each one of us has the capacity for a great love. Each one of us has a capacity to be a disciple, to follow someone who is worth following. With all our mind, with all our heart, with our whole being. How sad it would be if we do not find someone to whom we can give the best of ourselves, to give all of ourselves.

What would it be to have a king as a friend? Who is the person you most admire in your life? Who is the person in human history who has most fascinated you? Who is the person you'd like to meet someday, at least to see them up close, shake their hand, or to sit down and have a meal with face to face? Who has in some way inflamed your heart? Who is worthy of your life? Imagine: to have a friend who is a king!

There is a wonderful spiritual, "I'm Going to Meet the King." It's a very rousing hymn. Imagine how exciting: I'm going to meet the King!!! One of these days we'll be singing that as we go to meet the King of kings — each one of us. Even though Jesus has been with us every day of our lives, we rarely recognize Him.

The last Sunday of the liturgical year we dedicate to our King, to the One who has drawn us into His Kingdom, and has made us a holy people, a priestly people, a kingly people. We have royal blood. We are all of royalty. To follow back through our history, each one of us has been of kingly and queenly families somewhere (we have also been of slaves). In each one of us there is royal blood, and we experience each Sunday in the Eucharist that we receive the Royal Blood of Jesus Christ. But what difference does He make? Is Jesus really King? He doesn't claim that by power, although He could. It is up to each one of us to give Him power. He has no power except that which we give to Him by letting Him be decisive in our lives.

Who rules your heart? Who dominates your mind? What have you given of yourself this past week? this past year? Who really has power in your life? What do you consider number one? Is it your body, your clothing, your home, where you live, what you drive, the title you have behind your name? To what do you give your energy and time? To what do you commit your heart?

We have the capacity to worship. What is it to worship? Have you ever had an experience of worship, when you are so overwhelmed that you could do nothing but prostrate yourself? Have you ever been awed by another person? and want to follow that person come what may? What rules your life? If not your body, is it your senses, what you see and feel and touch and eat and covet? What do *you* want? What do you give? What do you give your beloved, your family, your parish? Or are you ruled by your mind, your intelligence, your cleverness? Who is most important in your life? Who absorbs and possesses you? To whom do you belong? Or in that deepest core of yourself, what dwells in you? Who dwells in you? Who has power over you? To whom do you give yourself?

"I'm going to meet the King!" Each one of us is on that journey and we will meet Him. He will look at each of us and say, "There is a kingdom prepared for you from the foundation of the world!" What are your credentials? Have you lived this kingdom all the days of your life? Have you recognized the King who is always hidden? He says, "I have been with you all the days of your life." And we will say, "When did we see you? When did we recognize you? When did we do anything for you?" Those who did something for the King perhaps didn't recognize it at the time; these are those who served the hidden Christ, the hidden King, in the stranger, in the foolish one, in the unattractive one. All of the Gospel, all of the kingdom, is summarized in those five words, "You did it to Me." If we don't heed them, then we have fallen. We kings and queens and princes and princesses, we have fallen. We rarely recognize it. We rarely get down to the depths of our being where we have the capacity to worship, to let go of everything, and to recognize Him in the least of our brothers and sisters.

Jesus said, "The kingdom of heaven is among you. The kingdom of heaven is within you." Where do we let Christ reign? If we do not give ourselves to Him, we give ourselves to things. We become more and more empty. What would it be if we could recognize and invite that hidden King to our table. In His presence we discover, in His light we begin to recognize those hidden facets of ourselves, that we are of royal blood, that we are holy people, priestly people, kingly people. Not as the world sees it. Our royalty gives us the capacity to serve, to give ourselves, to experience that the kingdom has begun in us.

Jesus is indeed a King. He is the King of our hearts. King of the Universe. We all long and hunger for someone to whom we can give ourselves totally and completely. We will never be able to do it, unless day by day we recognize Him in the people in our immediate lives and realize that in doing "it" to them we do it to Him.

THE LORD OF THE BANQUET

The word "God" is not distinctive of the Christian language; it belongs to all world religions. To be a Christian means that we claim to have Jesus' experience of God.

What is Jesus' experience of God? When you pray, to whom do you pray? To the Father? To the Son? To the Holy Spirit? Or, to whom it may concern?

Are we really Trinitarian? What makes us distinct from all world religions is that we believe that in God there are Three Persons. There are three who's to the what of God. We call this a "mystery." The more we know about a "mystery," the more wonderful, the more astonishing, the more inexhaustible that reality is. All the world religions believe in God, believe in a "what," but we are called to believe in a "who" — the Three "Who's" of the Trinity.

Most of us never act as Trinitarian but act as unitarians. Yet, the greatest gift that Jesus gave to us was in showing that He is not alone, and that we will never be alone. Jesus reveals that God is not simply a what, but God is the Who. God is a loving Father. All world religions know God as Creator, the Lord of the Universe, but Jesus revealed to us that we have a loving Father who is with us every day, gives us our daily bread. Our greatest human anguish is to be alone, unknown, unloved, unconnected. Jesus wants us to know His Father, to know that God is not lonely, to know that life in God is not lonely. The God that Jesus reveals is "Abba," a loving Father who cares for us. Not someone to be feared. Not someone always in judgment. Jesus revealed to us the intimacy of God. God is so immense, yet because He loves the world so much, there is no distance. He comes to each of us. We have Jesus' magnificent prayer: "I will come to you, and my Father will come to you, and we will make our home in you." God so loved the world, God so loves each of us, that He never leaves us. He never wants us to be alone. It is a fundamental teaching of Jesus, that we are like Him. As Jesus said, "I am never alone. The Father is always with me. I do nothing of myself. It is the Father living in me who is doing this, who is speaking this. All that I have learned of the Father, I am making known to you who are my friends."

Jesus spoke not only about His Father, but of someone else, an Advocate, a Comforter, His very own Spirit that He would send into us because there is so much that we do not understand. The Spirit will bring us to know, to understand. This is mind boggling. Do we dare to attempt to understand? Do we dare allow the Father, Son, and Holy Spirit within us to draw us into their experience. It is not enough to simply believe in God — all world religions do that. We are not disciples of Jesus unless we believe and live with the Father and the Son and the Holy Spirit. This mystery is given us not to confound our minds but to bring us into a new kind of consciousness, a new kind of life.

Do you have a sense of the Holy Trinity? Do you have an experience of God as Father? of Jesus as brother? of the Holy Spirit as power, as decision, as protest? It is so easy to become religiously numb. It is easy to stay in the childhood of faith and never to think, never to allow ourselves a sensation, a realization, a consciousness of what it is, what our faith says. God is a "what," an "it"; the Trinity is "who," "persons." Every one of us is called to experience a personal relationship to the Father, and to the Son, and to the Holy Spirit. God did not reveal the mystery of the Trinity as a dogma of faith, as simply something to believe on blind faith. Jesus has revealed these mysteries not only to expand our minds, but to expand our hearts. We are intended to experience what it is to worship. Do you ever allow yourself to be thrilled with God? to experience awe and wonder?

We so live from our habits. Habits can be very good, but they can numb us. We can do the right things without any reason whatsoever. Especially in our religious practice, we can remember the formula but forget the reality. So it is in our prayer. How often do we pray: "In the name of the..."? What, then, are we talking about? "In the name of the Father." What could we perhaps put in the place of "the name"? In the "communion" of the Father, Son and Holy Spirit. We so easily simply repeat the formula, but what is involved? Do you recognize the consecration, the offering of yourself, the power of the sign of the cross that you make over yourself again and again and again? Do you consciously bless yourself? Make yourself holy? Open yourself to God?

As we begin the liturgy, we always touch our hands to our head and say, "In the name of" — in the understanding of — "the Father," the mind of the universe. Our most fundamental experience of the Father should be one of being known and being understood. Who really knows you? Who really understands you — from the first moment of your existence? Who knows every one of your thoughts? every one of your actions? every breath?

What a joy to allow myself to experience that I am totally and completely known! I am understood. When I sign myself with the Trinity, and I touch my head, that is an act of faith that God knows and understands.

"...and of the Son." When I touch my heart, in the love of the Son, I recognize that I am loved by the Son of God, loved so much that He became one of us. He is always with us. We are always being loved. We affirm our knowledge that there is never a moment when we are not being loved. Even should we separate ourselves from His embrace, we will always be loved.

"...and of the Holy Spirit." Then we touch our shoulders, because we are not simply to know and to love, but to be launched into action through the power of the Holy Spirit — in our shoulders, and in our hands and in our feet. We become filled with the Holy Spirit enabling us to do the will of God.

And the will of God is our happiness and our fulfillment. But there is so much numbness in us. Psychic numbness. We so easily settle for the lowest level of consciousness. The mystery of the Trinity is not to dull our minds, but to expand our minds to an ever living consciousness that "I am never alone." That I am understood totally and completely. That I am invited to know myself as the Father knows me.

This mystery of the Trinity is not simply one of blind faith, but it is an invitation to exploration, to a personal, intimate relationship with the Father and with the Son and with the Holy Spirit because each of them is a Person. We are persons. We do not relate to a husband or wife as we do to our mother or father or brother or sister. Each relationship is intimate and unique. We are called to live an intimate, unique relationship with each Person of the Trinity as well. We are drawn to allow ourselves to experience "What is this reality that I call 'Abba,' Father?" "Who is this Jesus who is always coming to me?" "Who is He who cries out 'Live in me. Let me live in you!'"?

How deeply have you known your parents? It is sad how little we really connect in terms of our own father and mother at times, in terms of understanding them, knowing their mind and their heart. But Jesus knew His Father totally and completely, and He wants to give us that understanding, that knowledge. Jesus has given us His own Spirit, that we live no longer ourselves, but He lives in us. Do I dare to believe that within me is the mystery of God? Do I allow myself to recognize that I'm always called to expand my mind and heart? Just as we cannot get an ocean into a little bucket, we think we cannot get God into ourselves. But He comes to us and we become connected. We become holy people.

How many persons are there in you? Do you ever find yourself talking to yourself? Who are you talking to? Who is listening? We know from perhaps our catechism days the different images of the Trinity: St. Patrick with his shamrock, the three folds on the one flower. But there are so many different images of the Trinity. We have a mind. We have an intellect. We have a heart. We know things. What a wonderful thing intelligence is that we have the capacity to know. As our science today delves deeper into the exploration of the infinite universe or the sub-particle world, the more astonished we are of what the human mind can do. The human mind wants to take into itself everything there is to be known. What a thrill it is to discover and to understand!

One of our deepest human desires is to be known, to be understood. Who really knows you? Who really understands you? We are always looking for someone who knows and understands us — God is the one who knows and understands each of us. What a wonderful experience that is!

Likewise, it is only out of our intelligence that we can be activated to love. How do you love? How much do you love? What makes us distinctively human is our capacity to love. To give of our self. Married people have made vows to commit themselves to another person for the whole of their life. For better or worse, sickness and in death. But how easily that vow contracts and diminishes. How much we must own ourselves before we can really give ourselves. How few really know and own themselves.

How little we can give — but how wonderful when it happens — even if only for a moment or two. That we can give of our mind and of our heart, of our time, of our very being. What it is to love! This is the essence of what it is to be human. We all want to give our self totally and completely away. This is what Jesus has done. We want Him to be in us so that we can begin to love more and more and more.

The Gospel says, "God so loved the world that He gave us His only Son to be with us." He has so loved us that He could never say goodbye, so He is always in us. How much space does the Father, the Creator of the universe, need? What is your experience of God? How do you name the One who has created you and sustained you and keeps on drawing you further? My name for God is "Intimacy." God is so immense that He can make Himself almost nothing to come to be in me. He is closer to me than I am to myself.

The Father loves the Son so totally that His love becomes a person. The Son so loves the Father that it becomes a person. The image of man and wife becoming father and mother is similar: they love so much to bring forth a child, or 17 children. What is that human love? We are so small. Our capacity to know and understand is so fragile. Our capacity to love is so often at a minimal level, but what happens when Father, Son, and Holy Spirit come to us?

Why did Jesus reveal the Trinity? Because the Trinity is our future and our present.

How many persons are there in God? We say three: Father, Son, and Holy Spirit, but we forget that the Holy Trinity in some way is always drawing us into its reality. We are in the Trinity and the Trinity is in us.

How many persons are in you? There are four persons: you, the Father, Son, and Holy Spirit.

André Rublev, the great Russian holy man, one of the few artists recognized to be a saint, painted one of my favorite icons of The Blessed Trinity. Icons are those sacramentals which you look at long enough to allow the icon to look back at you. It is meant to create in you and to reflect to you your own holiness. Rublev took the image of the three persons appearing to Abraham and Sarah to tell Sarah that even though she was beyond the age of childbearing, she would bear a child, fulfilling the promise made to Abraham. Rublev's painting is of the Three Persons sitting around a small altar, and on the altar is a small chalice. That chalice is you. Imagine the work of the Holy Trinity: all they have to do all day and all night is to look upon you with love. You are in the center of the Trinity. The Trinity is in you and you live in the heart of the Trinity. They completely embrace us, and yet are within us. If we could only believe the truth — let our minds and hearts expand and ever seek the profound and deep experience of Father, Son, and Holy Spirit.

The Eucharist is always a prayer of the Trinity. It is Jesus in our midst offering Himself and all of us to the Father and calling upon the Holy Spirit to bring us to understand, to know, to love. Our Eucharistic Prayer concludes, "Through Him, with Him, in Him, in the unity of the Holy Spirit, all glory and honor is yours, almighty Father, for ever and ever." If we but knew the gift of God. If we'd dare to believe that each of us is holier than the altar, than the tabernacle, than the church because Father, Son, and Holy Spirit have come to us to fill our minds, our hearts, our whole being, making us the icon, the living sign of the presence of the Holy Trinity in the midst of this world.

It is easy to pour a drop of water into a chalice of wine. This is a simple act. But to pour a chalice of wine into a drop of water, the Divinity into humanity, that takes the love of the Three, Abba, Jesus, Spirit, for us. That takes the love of the Lord of the banquet, the Lord who invites you to the feast.

HERE I AM

Have you heard the Lord call you by name? Imagine what that experience would be like. We are not anonymous. We are not faceless before the Lord. He knows us because He created us, because He is our ultimate destiny. He knows each one of us by name. He is always loving us, always calling us.

Samuel was one of the first of the great prophets. He was to anoint the first King Saul and select David as the greatest king of Israel. His mother was Hannah and his father Elkanah. For years they had no children. Hannah wept because, as all Jewish women, she hoped she could be the one who would bear the Messiah. Elkanah came to her one day and he said, "Why are you weeping? Why do you not eat? Am I not more for you than ten sons?" What a beautiful, profound word of a husband to his wife who bore no children! "Am I not more than ten sons for you?" It was into that kind of family that Samuel was born. He was consecrated to the work of the Temple. In the night as Samuel slept, the Lord called him by name.

I've given a number of retreats for retired sisters and priests and I used to ask them, "What is the Lord's name for you? How does He call you by name?" Many said they couldn't believe that the Lord really knew them, that He called them by name. Few of us are known by name to the archbishop and the Holy Father, but Jesus knows your name. He is always calling you and inviting you.

Why do we so often fail to hear? How do we learn the language of God? How do we listen? Prayer is not simply talking. Prayer is most of all listening and being aware that the Lord is with us. Each one of us has experienced the Lord call us by name. In some way the Lord has called you and invited you. He desires a rendezvous with you. How many times each day the Lord calls us by name! He looks upon us with love and invites us to live more consciously in His presence.

Do you remember times when you have been awakened in the middle of the night? Do you recall times when you experienced a profound aloneness that is the reality of each of us? How we can feel alone! How we can feel unknown! There is something in the depths of ourselves that can never really be put into words. In our aloneness, we can experience a fullness as we realize that we are never really alone. We are never anonymous. We are never unloved. There is a deep instinct in each of us that we are drawn by God. He talks to us. We are invited to learn God's language, to understand more and more deeply who it is who is always in our lives. From the first moment of our conception to our last breath of life, God is our ultimate companion. Jesus is always with us, inviting us, nourishing us. If only we could open our ears and our heart to fully recognize the One from whom we have come and to whom we are going.

Recall the story of John the Baptist when he pointed out that the Lamb of God, the Servant of Yahweh, was passing by. Do you remember what happened? Two of his disciples immediately follow Jesus. What was it in those disciples, what was it in Jesus, that so readily drew them? Jesus knew that they were following Him — Jesus always knows where we are. And what did Jesus do? He turned to them and began His relationship with them by asking them a question: "What are you looking for?" What are *you* looking for? What do you seek today? What do you hunger for? There is a hunger for something more than food, for something more than sleep, for something even more basic. There is in each of us an immense capacity and hunger and desire for God even if we do not recognize it, even if we cannot name it.

When Samuel was called, he had not yet begun to know the ways of the Lord. God had not yet revealed Himself to Samuel, but the Lord is always revealing Himself to us. He's always teaching us. He's always stirring something up within us. Imagine what those two disciples, Andrew and John, experienced when Jesus turned to them and asked them that question: What are you looking for? They weren't aware of what they were looking for. They weren't aware of looking for anything. There was simply a tug within them to want to follow Jesus. They were wise enough then to ask Jesus a question: "Where are you? Where do you live?" Imagine Jesus' delight with that question! In response He gave them that double imperative: "Come and see." How many times we come to the Lord, how many times we read the Word, how many weeks we come to liturgy — and never "see." But the Lord continues to call us. He calls you this day to come and to see. To "taste and see," not "see and taste," but to "taste and see."

How does the Lord call you by name? How does He know you? How does He love you? You have a rendezvous with Him today. In every Eucharist He comes to you. He has already drawn you to Him. He comes to you and calls you by name. He knows you and gives you not only Himself, but a new gift of yourself. Listen. Do you hear the Lord call you by name? Do you pray for new ears and a new heart and a new hunger?

And so the wonderful story of Samuel is our story. Scripture is autobiographical; it always tells us about ourselves. How do we respond? The very same words God spoke to Samuel are used in the ordination of a priest. He is asked. He is called by name. His response is "Ad sum," "Here I am." These words were very poignantly lived by Archbishop Romero in Guatemala who always answered with the word, "*Presente*," "Here I am," "I render myself present." In every Eucharist we should try to render ourselves more consciously present. Not simply responding with the automatic "Amen," but once and while we should respond, "Yes, I am here." "*Presente.*" "I am giving myself in response to Your gift to me."

Let us dare to believe that the Lord is always with us, that He is always calling us by name, that He knows us, that He loves us. Let us dare to be like Samuel. "Here I am." "*Presente.*" Let us dare to be like Andrew and John to follow Jesus and to ask Him, "Who are you? Where do you live?" Recall that in meeting Jesus, Andrew was compelled to find his brother, Peter, and to bring him to Jesus. Jesus gave Peter a new name. Likewise, Jesus calls us to new consciousness, to new life, to a new name, to a new mission. Are you listening? Do you hear the Lord call you by name? Now respond: "Here I am. *Presente.*"

How Does He Call You By Name?

"I tell you, brothers and sisters, the time is short. From now on those with wives should live as though they had none, those who weep should live as though they were not weeping, and those who rejoice as though they were not rejoicing. Buyers should conduct themselves as though they own nothing and those who make use of the world as though they were not using it. For the world as we know it is passing away."
(1 Cor 7:29-31)

This is a rather strange reading. One Monday morning as I was reading it in preparation for Sunday's homily, I wondered how I could use this particular passage. Then, within the hour I heard of a serious earthquake in Los Angeles and a continuous series of quakes that followed upon that. At the same time in the news was concern for an Arctic ice age that seems to be wrapping itself around Detroit and the rest of the country.

Read these words again. Imagine our brothers and sisters gathered in the parishes of Los Angeles hearing this reading the Sunday following that devastating earthquake. Imagine how pertinent those words are, how much they describe what they had been living and would live for many months ahead.

Think of the Lord walking the shore of the Lake of Galilee and pointing His finger at particular people who were not expecting Him. He said, "Come. Follow me, and I will make you fishers of men." Are these words of two thousand years ago, or does Jesus walk in our midst today? and is He still calling us, inviting us, "Come. Follow me"? Did you hear His voice this week? Psalm 95 which begins the prayer of the Church each day says, "If today you hear his voice, harden not your heart... Listen to His voice today." How is your hearing? How does one hear the word of God? How does one recognize His presence? How do you improve your hearing? How do you pray?

The first moment of prayer is always listening. Each day we are called to listen because the Lord is with us. There is never a day that He doesn't draw us, attract us, give us a contemplative pause. To pray is to listen, to be ready, to respond. When you hear Him, you are drawn, tugged. He has a rendezvous with you. He has something to say to you, something to give to you. He will be in you and with you each day, each week.

I want you to close your eyes for a moment and just follow your breath into your inmost center that the psalmists speak of, the still point that is still in the midst of the whirling world. Listen now for the sound of your own name.

Everyone who says your name says it differently. Who is the one who, when they say your name, compels the little child within you to leap for joy? Whose call brings you delight and surprise, to feel expansive? Each time someone says your name, there is something of Jesus' voice in that sound.

How does the Lord call you by name? You're not a statistic or anonymous. He knows you. He loves you. He cares for you. There is no one who is not special. You are as significant as Abraham, as personally called as Moses, as important as David. Just as Jesus called Peter and John and Andrew and James in that walk along the shore, He is calling you. Jesus is always saying your name. Just as He called Paul on the road to Damascus, Magdalene at the tomb, Zacchaeus in the tree, so Jesus calls you, invites you. He knows you. He is always calling you to "a more abundant life." He calls you to awaken the gifts He has given you, for they are given not just for yourself, but for others as well.

Do you recognize your sphere of influence? Do you recognize that wherever you go, you make a difference? You may not say any word. Simply by your presence, by your faith, by your hope, by your love, you make a difference. Sometimes we forget: to be a disciple of Jesus is to know Him and to do what He tells us.

Jesus told us, "Pray that all may be one. There are many that are not yet part of this fold." He sent His disciples to the whole world commanding them to "teach them all that I have taught you." Jesus said, "I no longer call you servants. I call you friends, because everything I have learned from the Father I have made known to you, and because of this you are my friends. As the Father is loving Me, so I am loving you. As the Father is sending Me, so I am sending you."

If we could only believe the truth. We are called to more conscious life. We are called to be aware of Who it is we carry within ourselves. We are called to share our faith — what we have heard in darkness, we are to proclaim in the light; what we hear in whispers, we are to proclaim from the rooftops.

The time is very short. The world is changing in ways we can't imagine. Every one of us has a vocation. We have a call. We are called to recognize Who it is that walks in our midst, to not harden our hearts, to know that what we have been given is not to remain with ourselves. How many have you drawn, invited? A significant percentage of the people signed up as members of our parishes no longer come. Many are waiting for an invitation. I've knocked on door after door many times in my ministry. Many people said, "I didn't realize what I was doing. I simply drifted away. No one even remembered my name. No one ever came, knocked on my door, called me on the phone and said 'I miss you'."

How many are waiting? Each of us has a vocation. Each of us has a sphere of influence. There are so many waiting for us to call them by name, as we have been called by name. They wait for us to share what has been given to us — what they are waiting for: Jesus, the Lord.

Do I Ever Really Say Yes?

Have you ever had the experience of an angel? Would you want to have one? You don't expect it. You don't look for it. But imagine what happened to Mary, a young woman perhaps just occupied in her normal day, sitting there anticipating nothing, or she may have been scrubbing the floor, she may have been preparing a meal. An angel from God came to her. It seems unreal. We accept it because we have heard it so often, but what an incredible moment! What would be the experience of an angel coming to you? Some suggest that the angels were sent to everyone when Jesus was born, but that only the shepherds were able to see and hear them. Everyone else was so busy with other things. How many times has an angel been sent to you, but you were not ready, did not hear or see? I have a suspicion that many times before Mary angels were sent, but no one was ready, no one listened, no one saw — until Mary. Mary recognized God's "yes" to humankind and Mary said her "yes," and everything has been irrevocably changed.

What if I were to say to you, "An angel is going to come to you this week"? Are you ready? What is the experience of the holy? of the sacred? of the mysterious? I think most of us have good leaden shields. We've all had x-rays and experienced the shields placed over us to prevent damage. So often, in our minds and our hearts, we have our own kind of leaden shields which prevent anything new or extraordinary from happening to us.

Did you ever wish for an angel? or pray for an angel? Are we so comfortable with the ordinary and the everyday that we do not hear, we do not see, we do not change. It takes so much energy to listen, to act, and to change. How long does it take to experience anything? We are bombarded with so much media, we almost have to insulate ourselves from getting caught in it. Perhaps we insulate ourselves too much. How rare it is that we really hear the word of God! Does it ever touch us? Do we really receive the Eucharist? Does it really make any difference?

How long does it take to experience reality? When I visited Jerusalem and Bethlehem, I used to take three hours at every site, just to sit, to try to understand, to in some way get into what happened in Bethlehem, or in Nazareth, or Jerusalem. It was never long enough. Three hours — what's three hours? What were Jesus' three hours on the cross?

Imagine the Annunciation. Imagine what happened. The most important moment of our liturgical year is not Christmas. That simply makes visible what happened nine months earlier: the Incarnation, God becoming human. Liturgically we don't even celebrate the feast. Perhaps it is too much. Perhaps it is beyond our comprehension. We can understand a child being born. We can see it. But that God could become human…!

Imagine the reverse of the big bang theory, the theory that since that first moment of creation, energy has been expanding at the rate of 186,000 miles per second. But when that energy runs out, then all the universe as we know it is going to be pulled back into itself by the force of gravity. There would be a compression of all that we know down to the smallest particle of matter. Now, imagine God of the universe, in all His power and infiniteness, His immensity, becoming almost nothing in order to enter into our lives. More understandably He could have come as a full grown man or woman or even a child. But for God to become a cell, an ovum, almost nothing… and to believe that this has happened. There is no way we can put our minds and our hearts around that so we tend not to think about it. But imagine what would happen if instead of trying to get a nicer home or a larger home, a better car or a bigger car, a more significant, a more prestigious job. Imagine looking for a smaller house, a littler car. Imagine so reducing yourself as to live in a tent. Can you imagine? We are people of the up-escalator. It's hard to imagine going down the up-escalator. It's hard to imagine being unemployed until you are unemployed. But the poverty of God emptying Himself out, how can we understand that? that God has come to us? Not for a moment, but to live in us. To root Himself in us. To be more than an almost invisible point in our life, more than a thought or an idea. To begin the "big bang" all over again. To, in some way, penetrate our hearts, our minds, our hands, our feet so that we would become what He is, that we would become poor, that we'd begin to recognize that every person we see is our brother or our sister.

It is not easy to be ready. So many haven't any clue what the Incarnation is all about. Are we ready to say our "yes"? Are we ready to become little? Are we ready to let go? How long does it take for a thought or an idea to penetrate the shields we have all around us? How long does it take to change? Every time that we pray the Creed, we are invited to bow our heads, "...and the Word was made flesh." On Christmas Eve, we pause and kneel for a moment, look at the crib and wonder, but we forget. It's hard to hold on to.

Do we allow ourself to be touched by the mystery of God? Jesus so often said, "If you but knew the gift of God and who it is that speaks to you, that lives in you...." When we receive the Body and Blood of Christ, when we witness once more, "This is My Body given for you. This is My Blood that continues to be shed for you," we demonstrate the mystery of our faith. Mystery of love. Mystery of a "yes."

It is so easy to celebrate Christmas and totally miss it. It's so important to stop, to think, to in some way dare to be in awe and wonder that in one moment Mary said "yes" and nothing would be the same again. Each of us is invited to say a new "yes," one that was never said before. There's so much within us that is not yet born. Christmas, the Incarnation: Mary took nine months, that's a long time — and what a "yes" she said. To the angel she said the first "yes." The rest of her life was a more difficult "yes."

To each of us an angel comes. Jesus Himself, Body and Blood, comes to us. He is waiting for something. Our lives will have meaning, significance, value, only if we recognize the angel and give our "yes."

Come to Your Melting Point

When does your heart burn within you? What gets you excited and enthused? What makes you want to hold on to that experience? Do you recognize when the Lord has touched you?

Have you had an Emmaus experience? Are you like that couple on the road with Jesus? Something prevented them from seeing Jesus. There's always so much to prevent us from seeing Him. He always so quickly disappears.

I woke up at 5:00 one morning, and my heart was burning within me. I was so excited that I couldn't sleep, just with the joy of being with friends again after a long absence.

How long does it take to absorb the presence of another person? How long does it take to get to know someone? It takes a time. When I last traveled to Jerusalem, I went to Emmaus three times. The seven mile walk takes three hours. We're not sure exactly where the Emmaus of Jesus' day was. There are four that claim the site. I went to each of them and lingered there.

In Jerusalem, I was called to linger at many sites. I remember visiting the Holy Sepulchre at Calvary. So many tourists came in for only two minutes. They took their picture and moved back to the bus. But something happened to me there. It was as if I heard the words, "Don't go. Stay. Stay a little while." I remembered that Jesus spent three hours hanging on Calvary, and I felt compelled to spend at least three hours there. That became my little tradition: to go and just sit, for three hours, simply to try to experience, to remember, to let something be awakened, fired in me.

I did that in Bethlehem where Jesus was born. This was a funny experience because there was a group taking a lot of flash pictures. This distracted me. I had been reading my Bible, and I raised my eyes to see what so attracted them. They were taking pictures of me, this old man with the beard reading his Scripture! It was a new experience of myself!

What is the Emmaus experience? Do you remember certain moments when your heart was compressed in some way and you experienced it burning within you, when you didn't want to let go of it? What we hear of in the Emmaus story is something we have all experienced. So often we don't recognize it. We don't recognize Jesus.

These disciples, probably a husband and wife, were going in the wrong direction. They were going away from Jerusalem. They probably had seen Him on the cross, crucified, dead. And everything that they had earlier heard and hoped seemed to no longer make sense. So they were on their way home. They walked *away* from Jerusalem. They walked away from Jesus. They walked away from the Church. They walked away from their hope. The amazing thing is that Jesus followed them. We rarely follow Jesus, but He is always following us. He caught up with them, and He engaged them in conversation. They asked Him whether He didn't know what had been going on. He asked, "What things?", and He walked and talked with them. As He unfolded the Scriptures to them, their hearts began to burn within them.

What does it take for our hearts to get warmed up, to move from the pilot light of our baptism to a fire that overflows. Jesus said, "I have come to cast fire." How long does it take to melt us, to enkindle something in us? Yes, we need the Emmaus experience. Again and again.

How many would claim to have had the Emmaus experience? How many would claim that something, at one time or another, has been enkindled within? How many claim to *know* Him in whom they believe? It should be all. Every one of us. Perhaps we have no words to express our experience. This is why Jesus comes to us again and again and why we have forty days to celebrate Easter, fifty days with Pentecost.

I have that very intimate moment of giving others the Body and Blood of Christ. I see them at the door as they leave. I take some of their hands. Those I know embrace me because I've had an Emmaus experience with them. I celebrate two Eucharists each weekend, but I have four Emmaus experiences each week. ("Emmaus" is another way of describing PRH, Personality and Human Relations. It means taking the time to receive the gift of oneself.) An hour is not enough. How long does it take to absorb the presence of a person? How long does it take to really be at home? I think most of us shortchange ourselves. I like a long liturgy. I would love to give a fifty minute homily. There's not enough time.

I have a gift. I can take people to Emmaus. I have a gift to help people receive the gift of themselves, to come to know who it is that is living deep within them, who is always waiting for us. I'd like to take you to Emmaus.

Most of us give very little time to ourselves. We don't believe we are worth our own time. Most of us have spiritual anorexia, we are really spiritually starving because we feed ourselves so little. This is why Jesus is always coming after us. He is always knocking on the door, not outside, but within us, deep within us. He's always saying (do you ever hear Him saying), "Don't go"? Do you hear Him say, "Stay. Stay with me"? Do you allow yourself to listen to Him? You don't have to go to the Holy Land. I've been there and I've received some of the fire. I've climbed Mt. Sinai. I walked at the foot of Mt. Hermon, a thousand miles north of Sinai where Jesus took His disciples to Caesarea Philippi. Everywhere that Jesus walked, I tried to walk in His steps. I have received that to share. I have something to give. My retreats, days of prayer, and PRH sessions bring me to companions for the Emmaus journey. We share something of one another. We have something to give. I think that you have something to give as well.

Those people who have taken the Emmaus journey with me don't shake hands, we always embrace. It's no prejudice that we shake hands with others, but once you've made the Emmaus journey, you can no longer be strangers.

Jesus does not want to remain at a distance. He wants us to know Him. He wants the little child in us to leap for joy. He wants to enkindle in us an immense fire, not just for ourselves, but to overflow into many. Jesus is already in each of us. Do you recognize His presence in you? Do you want Him to grow so that He overflows from you into others? We are a holy people, but most of our halos are pretty well concealed. We need to take time to let our hearts be enkindled. Some of us have a very high melting point. Some have never allowed Him to melt them, perhaps have never taken the time to listen to His invitation, "Don't go. Stay with me."

I'd like to lead you to Emmaus. I can promise to take you there. I can promise you an experience of yourself that you've never had before. I can help you to find the way into your heart and to let it begin to burn.

It took the Emmaus couple three hours to walk from Jerusalem. They were tired. It's not an easy walk. But once they had met Jesus, and recognized Him in the breaking of the bread, and in the Eucharist, they were compelled to immediately walk back to Jerusalem to share their joy with their Christian community. That is the Easter experience! That is what we are called to become.

I pray that your melting point be reached, that you allow your heart to burn within you, that you feel compelled to recognize the Jesus in you, to recognize the Jesus in one another. "If you but knew the gift of God." — You do *know* it. But it's not enough to know, you must allow yourself to be enkindled.

Come to Emmaus. Let us walk together.

Have You Seen the Star?

Did you? Did you see the star? Were you looking for it? Were you ready to follow it? What gifts would you have brought?

Epiphany means "manifestation." The manifestation of God's Son to the whole world. Someone said about the end of the holiday season, "Well, this kind of wraps it all up." But no, it is just the beginning.

What was within the magi, within the men or women who came looking for something, perhaps all of their lives. They were learned people, and they knew something would happen. They saw the star at its rising, and they immediately followed it. We have no idea where they came from. We do not know how many there were. We hear about the three gifts. Perhaps some came from Africa, some from China, some from India. Perhaps each started all by themselves, but these individuals converged. They came. They followed the star. They found the Child. They adored Him. They offered Him their gifts.

What star are you following? What are you looking for? The Lord God is always manifesting Himself, showing Himself, revealing Himself. The word epiphany also implies transparency — to catch a glimpse of God. What have been your epiphanies? What have been the triggers, the people and things, through which you catch a glimpse of God?

Some have said that the "big bang," through which the universe came into being, is still going on. If we would listen deep within ourselves, we'd hear the echo of the big bang, the first moment of creation, because each of us is, in some way, stardust. Do you know where you have come from? in the beginning? Do you know where you are going? Where are you on the journey?

Did you follow the star? Did you really meet Jesus this Christmas?

All the gifts have now been put away or exchanged. All that you have received and that you have given. In most Catholic countries the Epiphany is the gift-giving day, not December 25. This is the most important feast of the entire season. The Epiphany is the first celebration of the mystery of Jesus. What did you receive from Him? What did you give? What happened this Christmas with regard to the Christmas "ring" around your life? How have you been changed? What did you see? What did you hear? What gift of yourself were you able to give?

Of the magi, we hear that they came and *adored*. How do you adore? How do you "do" adoration? Did you kneel for a moment at the crib? or, far more importantly, at the tabernacle? How do you pray? What did you come here this morning to do? What gifts are you bringing today? What gift of your mind, of your heart? What will happen this week of this year? Have you drawn up your five year plan for the third millennium? How do you adore? offer? give? "gift" yourself? What is He waiting for? Do you know the gift that you are? Do you ever allow yourself to be excited with what you have received, in order that you may give? God is total giving. He is always giving, even more than the sun that is burning itself out each day. God is always giving everything to each of us. We are the image and likeness of God to the degree that we become "gift," that we are giving. What gifts do we have to give?

Do you realize that you have seen the star? Otherwise, you would not be drawn as you are. You are a believer. You come to Mass to offer at least an hour of your week, to offer your work, your prayer, your family. You are the magi. Not the magi of two thousand years ago, but each of you has in some way seen the light and heard the invitation. You respond. You come to adore. It is not over. It is not all wrapped up. It is just beginning. The greatest epiphany is the Eucharist, what we do together when we gather for Eucharist, recognizing the Body and Blood of Christ, that He is still with us, and that He is still on a journey, and that there is a long way for each of us to go.

I recently visited with the family of a couple I've known for over thirty years. They have nine children, and I talked with each one of them. Not one of these children goes to Church today. The seven who are married have had thirteen different marriages. The light has gone out in them. I've never seen a more beautiful light than in the father and mother, but somehow during the 1960's and 1970's the light has gone out for their children. None of the nine has a conscious faith. I think they are all believers. I know that each one of them is on a journey. Each is looking and struggling and suffering, trying to find that light. The light is already in them, but they do not know it.

You are holy people, blessed people, because you have swallowed a star. It is in you. You come Sunday after Sunday because you believe, but do you know what an incredible gift that is? It doesn't just happen. It is not passed on automatically through the sacraments. We have to look for it and be faithful to it — just as we have to pray. If we don't pray, the light goes out. Keeping the light takes time. It requires the realization that everything we have is total gift. It means we have to keep on giving. Faith is not a matter of words or ideas or thoughts. It is a life. "Epiphany" is Jesus saying, "Hear my word. Take and eat my Body and Blood. Become an epiphany. Become transparent. Become incandescent." How many will you encounter this week whose only light is going to be your faith? They walk in your light. They walk in your faith. They walk in your joy. How many of you have a community, are a community? How important is it that you pray, that you adore, that you absorb again and again the light of the star? You absorb it so deeply that it becomes radiant. It radiates because of your faith, because of your becoming "gift." We are most like Him when we give ourselves more and more to others.

Have you seen the star? Dare to say, "Yes. I have seen the star. I have swallowed the star. I have made the journey. And now I am sent in a new way to be an epiphany, to be a light, to be a joy, to be a hope."

How many are waiting to see the light? How many await the gift that we carry within ourselves for them?

Are You Ready?

WHERE ARE YOU IN THE GOSPEL?

In one parable (Mt 25:14-30), Jesus tells us of the master who, preparing for a trip, entrusts his property to three of his slaves. These are held accountable for their use of the talents bestowed on them. It is a rather heavy parable. It is rather serious to realize that we will be held accountable.

Where do you find yourself in the Gospel? With whom do you identify? Are you the one who was given the 5000, the five talents? the one with the 2000, the two talents? or the one with the one talent, the 1000? The last, we are told, did not live up to his master's expectations.

What are your talents? What have you done with the gifts that have been given to you? There are some talents that we are compelled to develop in order to survive, make a living. We usually take care of ourself. We all have a "talent" for that. We take care of our families, usually because we don't have too much choice there either. These demands are set. But there are talents, perhaps the ones we are least aware of, those most hidden, that we do the least with. We are made not only for ourselves, for our families, but each one of us is a member of humanity. Each one of us is a member of a city, a town, a state, a country, a world. We are connected to others. We are connected to one another. Often this is the talent least developed. It's rather embarrassing that those who have been given the most materially and intellectually, so often do not develop the talent of the heart, the talent of compassion.

Perhaps it's almost in proportion: that which we achieve on one level, we lose on the other level, the most important level.

We are not equal. We do not come from equal backgrounds. We do not have equal opportunities. We do not have equal talents. There is a wide diversity. There is a great variety in distribution of the good things of life. This suggests a redistribution of wealth, a redistribution of pain. So many have a "right" to the good things we have, but they often go without because we are so caught up in ourselves or our family. We too easily think we have done all we can do. But Jesus, again and again, breaks into our life with a word intended to wake us, to disturb us.

There are some who no longer come to church, not because they are not getting something out of it, but that they don't want to be reminded, they don't want to be disturbed. They have closed themselves off to the Word. Many come who don't listen to the Word. We don't always realize that it is good to allow ourselves to be disturbed, to be awakened, to know that Jesus is always calling us beyond where we are. You can be sure that He intends to keep at us until we discover our hidden talents, our hidden gifts. Then we will realize that they are not just for ourselves or for our families, but for all. Our gifts are also intended for those who have not "made it," those whose "little that they have" is continually being taken away from them.

What the Gospel does is reflect reality. Those who have, take more and more. Those who don't have, have less and less. Even in our country. Even those of our faith.

What is your most important talent? What will you have to say to the Lord in terms of all He has given to you? Each one of us has a talent. Each one of us has a gift that makes us like God. We have the capacity to love. We have the capacity to believe. We have the capacity to hope. In the Gospel story of the talents, no one sinned. No one did anything wrong. It was a matter of what the person failed to do. Perhaps our greatest sin is "omission," what we did not do, what we did not see.

In Matthew's Gospel, chapter 25, on the day of the final judgment, we will be judged by what we did or failed to do to the Lord. When the apostles heard this, they cried out, "When were you poor? When were you sick? When were you a stranger? When were you alone?" They hadn't recognized Jesus in others. They did not know Him in the faces of the needy.

Recall Jesus' terrible words to Peter, "Depart from me because I do not know you." How will Jesus get to know us? Not by our simply taking care of ourselves, by taking care of our families, by taking care of our necessities. There is always more required than that. Jesus is always asking us for *more*.

"Come. Follow me." I am always disturbed when I hear those words, "Sell all that you have. Give it to the poor. And come, follow me." I know very few who have sold *all* that they have, but each one of us *can* let go of a little that we have. We don't need all that we continue to claim. What is the Lord calling us to do or to become? This past week, how did you use your talent of love? Who did you see this week? Who did you take time for? We're always so busy, but how many people in our life, in our own family haven't heard from us in a long time? Did we work at developing that talent of love, that talent of compassion, that talent of joy, that talent of faith. To whom did you give yourself this week? Whom did you remember? Everyone needs a little time, a little appreciation, a little admiration. How rarely do we tell even the people in our own family of our gratitude, our affection, our need!

Everything that the world needs has already been given to it. We have the capacity to end material poverty. We have the capacity to end war. It hasn't happened because so many have not developed their deeper talents, their deeper gift, their gift of peacemaking, of living out the beatitudes. We can say we have kept the commandments. They belong to all world religions. But Jesus has given us the beatitudes, the way of happiness, the way of compassion, the way of personal presence to others. The sign that we receive the Eucharist is not our knowledge that Jesus is with us, but our realization that Jesus is calling us and sending us to be His presence to others. What we do to the least of His brothers and sisters is what we do to Him. That invitation continues. The call is there. We may have done wonderful things with some of our talents, but what Jesus is talking about is our most important talent, the most important gift: to love one another as He has loved us. Whatever our gift, whatever we have been given, we lose if we do not make it a "gift." The only thing we can take with us is what we have given to others, in terms of our time, in terms of our presence. The hour is coming when we can no longer work. We must store up for ourselves treasures in heaven, the ones in the bank we will not take with us. It is only what we do for the little ones that is our treasure in heaven. Let us pray that we will recognize our deeper and hidden talent, that when the Lord returns, He will say, "Well done. Come. Enter into the joy of your master."

"I CAN'T WAIT"

"For me, life is Christ." How long did it take Paul to experience that life is Christ and to be so drawn that he would say, "I long to die and be with Him"? Where are you in that journey? How much do you hunger and yearn? What are you looking for? What is it to be lifted into Christ?

Scripture tells us of the lord of the vineyard going out six times seeking workers: at dawn, at midmorning, at noon, afternoon, late afternoon, and, finally, in the evening. How many times has the Lord come to you and invited you to move beyond where you are? At every stage of our life, even though we do not seek or look for Him, He comes to us — at every stage of our life: at the dawn of our life, midday, at noon time... and so often we are not ready. So often we have not delved deeply enough into ourselves.

How sad it is to be a cradle Catholic all of our lives — to never get out of the crib, simply to be fed and changed. There are so many who never get out of the crib. Some begin to grow a little. Some begin to ask questions — but so often the search is crowded out by other things. So many are spectators: one of a vast multitude. How few take the next step! Where are you in that journey? Do you long to die and be with Christ? Or does that sound like nonsense?

I remember meeting John LeClerc in Oxford, England. He is a Benedictine writer on the spiritual life who has written over 700 books and articles. I asked him, "How do you pray?" He shrugged his shoulders and said, "I pray all the time or I never pray."

Somehow that did not satisfy me, and, as I pushed him further, he responded, "Well, I'm in my 70's now and I don't need as much sleep as I used to. So every night I have time to think about God. And *I can't wait.*" ... I can't wait. What is your hunger for life? For a more abundant life? A more meaningful life? So often we are so satisfied with so little. So many of us have spiritual anorexia. We are spiritually starving, and we don't even know it.

How do you hear the Gospel? How do you prepare yourself to receive the Word of God? Are you anxious, hungry, yearning to receive something special? It is not easy to hear the Word. Perhaps it is more difficult than ever before in our history. Now, more than ever, we are bombarded with so much, so many words, so much information that perhaps it is rare to really hear anything. Preparing oneself for the Word of God gives us meaning, direction, and joy in our life. "Seek the Lord while He may be found. Call Him while He is near" is a song we frequently sing at Mass. In his first letter to the Thessalonians, St. Paul tells them that he has no desire to place restrictions or burdens on them, but that he wanted to promote what is good, what would help them to devote themselves entirely to the Lord.

I often wonder what people take home with them from a liturgy, what they gather, what stays with them. Years ago, many families met for family breakfast after Mass each week. As the family gathered, a parent would ask, "What did Father talk about this morning?" Usually the children would remember. They had better! They were trained to. Families used to discuss the Gospel. Have you ever experienced that? What if we provided people with notebooks on their way into church so they might jot down some notes?

Since Vatican II we have a three year cycle of Gospel readings. One year we have Matthew's Gospel; another year, Mark; another year, Luke. John is intermixed throughout each year. It is helpful to recognize which Gospel you hear, to understand the distinctiveness of each Gospel. Can you distinguish Matthew from Mark, Luke from John? Have you read any of the Gospels straight through? You might start with Mark's. It is the shortest of the Gospels, only 16 chapters, about 30 pages. You could read it slowly in about an hour. It is rewarding to read a whole Gospel at one sitting. It can be fruitful to jot down how a particular Gospel speaks to you, or to recognize how much of it you already carry within yourself, or to record from memory how much of the Gospel has imprinted itself in you.

Suppose we lost all the Gospels. What would we remember? What do we cherish within ourselves? What would you list as your ten favorite lines of the Gospel? In some way, what you remember is who you are and what you are called to become. Why does some verse of the Gospel really penetrate such that you can never forget it? What is your most embarrassing line of the Gospel? The most uncomfortable one? For me it is, "Sell all that you have. Give it to the poor. Come follow me." These imperatives haunt me. They embarrass me.

What is your favorite line of the Gospel? If you were to take one line of all that Jesus has said, what would it be? What do you hang on to? What nourishes you? What gives you life? I have engraved along the lips of my chalice, "I am the vine. You are the branches. Without me you can do nothing."

What tends to come through to you? What stays with you? What feeds you? What are you ready to receive? "We should know the Gospels as we know our own hand," says Frank Sheed in *Theology and Sanity*. Are there passages you recognize? Can you remark, "That's Mark," or "That's Luke," or "That's Matthew," or "That's John"?

Have you stepped out of your cradle? Do you give yourself time to grow, to nurture yourself with the Word? When He comes next dawn, and noon, and evening, how ready will you be to receive Him?

YES, I AM

"Whoever eats my flesh and drinks my blood will live in me and I in them, says the Lord." (Jn 6:56)

Corpus Christi — the Body of Christ. Can you remember before Vatican II how you came to the altar to receive communion? As the priest stood before you, he would say to you, "Corpus Christi," and your response would be, "Amen." That literally means, "Yes, I am — the body of Christ." What makes us distinctively Catholic is faith in the Eucharist, that the presence of Christ is not simply on the altar and in the tabernacle. Christ's presence is in us. We dare to say, "Yes, I am — the body of Christ."

Some of us were taught that our Lord comes and stays with us only as long as the appearance of the bread and the wine remains in us, and that then Jesus is no longer there. That was not adequate teaching. When a person comes and stays with us for a while and then moves away, doesn't something of their presence linger with us? Whenever we meet someone, they make an imprint upon us. They deposit something of their life in us and it continues to be in us.

Now we understand the Eucharist more fully, that Jesus comes to us in each celebration not to disappear in a few moments, but to live in us continuously and more fully. Something of Jesus is imprinted upon us, deposited in us. We come to see that with every Eucharist we are somehow different, changed into a new being.

One of the amazing things about the Eucharist is that it is our proof of a different kind of food. The more we receive Jesus, the hungrier we become. That is one sign that we are growing in our devotion, in our awareness that we are the body of Christ. We develop an immense hunger bringing us to Mass, not only on Sunday but every time we have the chance. We realize how much we need to be fed, to taste and see. What a gift that is, to be able to receive the Body and Blood of Christ! What a strange paradox, that the more we receive, the hungrier we become.

Until Vatican II, not very many people received Communion every Sunday. We had a deep belief that we had to be worthy — at least we thought we did — to receive our Lord. We tried to go to Confession so that we would be as ready as possible, as open as possible, as sin-free as possible, to receive the Body and Blood of Christ. But we know that we can never be fully worthy to receive the Body and Blood of Christ. We come to the table because we need Jesus, because we are hungry for love.

It seems surprising that the more people receive Eucharist on Sunday, the fewer who seem to come to Mass during the week. We need to ask when we receive Eucharist: Is our devotion stronger? Is our understanding deeper? Do we really understand what it is all about? The feast of Corpus Christi is a strong reason, a timely opportunity, to meditate and to contemplate the gift we are offered in each Eucharist.

Do you ever wonder about those priests of old when everyone brought something up to the altar to be sacrificed? Imagine what it would be like to slaughter a bullock around the altar and to catch the blood of that ox, to sprinkle one half of it around the altar. The priest would come down from the altar and scatter and splatter the people assembled with that blood. Most of us would go under our pews to hide! So many are even shy of holy water, never mind blood! Yet there is something terribly real about blood, especially if it is our own blood. For those who give blood transfusions, it is an amazing moment to see your blood disappearing.

When you cut yourself and blood spurts forth, a certain awe and horror of blood arises in us. This is because blood is life.

Jesus speaks in such a graphic and realistic way: "Unless you eat my body and drink my blood, you cannot have life in me." Jesus is trying to tell us how totally He comes and gives Himself to us. We do not diminish Him, we do not change Him as we change our other food into ourselves. The whole point of the Eucharist is that when we receive the Body and Blood of Jesus, *we are changed* to become more like Christ. It is not a figure of speech when we say to "Corpus Christi — Body of Christ," "Yes — Yes, I am."

The Gospel tells us that in the bread and wine, Jesus takes, blesses, breaks, and gives Himself to us. This is the heart of the Eucharistic prayer. What can Jesus take if we do not give it to Him? Why are we drawn to the table, to be listeners, spectators? Or, do we realize that every one of us comes to offer sacrifice, to offer ourselves, to render ourselves present? We know that in the Eucharist, Christ is always rendered present, not in past time but right now in risen glory. Jesus' love is rendered present for us, is always there. Yet, Christ's presence in us depends so much upon us, upon our hope and our love, upon what we are doing with our lives. How much energy does it take to give our attention to Jesus? to render ourselves present, to say "yes," not just in a ritualistic way, but to say "YES" to who Jesus is in us?

We are called to be open and to pray. Eucharist draws us to an awesome transformation, a conversion. Do you remember the word "transubstantiation"? Transubstantiation: the bread and wine are changed into Jesus. There is nothing left of the bread and wine except the outward appearances. Jesus is to be present sacramentally; that means more than physically. Jesus is there for us. A kind of ongoing transformation, a transubstantiation, is happening in us because HE IS IN US and we are to be changed in our minds and our hearts. Every time we receive, we receive the capacity to render ourselves more present, to say a deeper "Yes." In this way, Jesus takes what we have, what we are willing to give, and blesses it. Jesus blesses us, embraces us (to bless is to embrace), and draws us to Himself like little children. "Unless you become like little children...." There is no way of receiving the Eucharist except as a little child.

We will never understand adequately what Jesus is saying. So we believe in the faith of the Church for two thousand years that Christ is here with us, taking us, blessing us, breaking us. Are we aware that there is no point in being Christian, no point in being Catholic, if we do not know that life will break our hearts, that people will break our hearts. If our heart is not broken, then there is no room for anyone, anything, except ourselves.

When we celebrate the Feast of the Sacred Heart, the human heart in Jesus, we acknowledge with gratitude that heart broken, poured out for us, that heart open to receive us again and again. Jesus breaks us, opens us up, frees us. He frees us from ourselves. As He begins to give us, to pass us around, we become sacrament. The focus is not simply on the altar and in the tabernacle; the great breakthrough of Vatican II is that the focus is upon us! Energized and filled with Jesus, we can go forth to be His body, His blood, His joy, His sacrament wherever we go. We carry Christ within ourselves, a truth so overwhelming that it is hard for us to hold. Like a falling star in the night, we are not even sure we saw it. But what a gift! If you but knew the gift of God and who it is that lives within you, who it is that sends you forth. You are the altar. You are the tabernacle.

Once, on Corpus Christi, as we followed the Body of Christ in procession around the parish, one of the neighborhood children became excited and called out, "Do you do this every Sunday?" Yes. There is a Corpus Christi procession every Sunday, but it is not as a crowd. As individuals and as families, we do the Corpus Christi procession to our homes, to our neighborhoods, to the office and the factory. Wherever we are, we are Corpus Christi.

Do you dare to say as Jesus offers Himself to you, as people ask you who you are, "I am Corpus Christi, the Body of Christ."

Can you say, "Yes. I am," in such a way that people know that Jesus is in you, that the body of Christ is in us?

May each one of us pray for a stronger devotion and a deeper awareness of what it is to be the body of Christ. May we be aware that every time we receive the Body and Blood of Christ, each one of us becomes a whole procession: sacrament, light, love, to be shared with others.

With the Company of Heaven

"He came to Nazareth, where He had been brought up, and went into the synagogue on the Sabbath day as He usually did." (Lk 4:16)

After being tempted in the desert, Jesus returned to His home town. What must it have been like when Jesus came home for the weekend? You can imagine the excitement and celebration of His neighbors — that Jesus was coming home. "Hometown boy makes good." They have heard from all different sides about this wonder-worker. For thirty years He had been in their midst and no one recognized Him. Then, all of a sudden, Jesus became the most spoken of person in the whole area. So you can imagine that Sabbath day when He came to the synagogue.

One of the great gifts of Judaism was that all the men were literate. Each person had an equal responsibility to celebrate Yahweh. They had the scrolls in an ark much like our tabernacle. They did not come of age until they could read. The test of one's manhood was to stand up and be able to read the Word of God. So it was natural that Jesus would unroll the long scroll and begin to read. He did not simply pick up the scroll at random, however. Scripture tells us, "He found His passage in the scroll." He found His place, just as each one of us is to find our place in the Word of God. Have you found your place, your call? Do you know who you are? For what has God made you? For what has God gifted you with all your talents? The Word of God is our story. It is our family's history. It is our autobiography. It is our mirror.

I have often thought how wonderful it would be if each person could find their place in the Word of God and then come to celebrate it with the community saying, "This is me. I've found my script. I've found my place. I know my lines." The Word of God is a kind of manuscript, a script for us to live out. Jesus knew who He was and He lived it out. The script is still there and the players are called forth — not to play, but to live.

The story of Luke is a good place for us to begin to look and search for our roles, for our call, for what we are intended to become. Jesus knew. He not only knew, He prayed over it. What a moment for Jesus when He came to stand before the people. Even though He had been with them so long a time, they did not know Him. Still, Jesus dared to stand up and to proclaim who He is. How crucial for us to take the time to pray over ourselves, over our cities, our country, our world. Only through the Word spoken in the silence of our hearts will we, like Jesus, be able to proclaim who we are. If Jesus needed to take time out to pray, how much more do we need to take time out to pray!

To pray is to claim that we are not alone. St. Paul said, "Together we are the body of Christ." In each one of us, Jesus has poured something of His Spirit. In each one of us, Jesus has deposited a gift that is incomparable to anyone else's gift. The great call of Vatican II is that we begin to recognize who we are, that the Church is not just the religious. Ninety-nine percent of the Church is ordinary, everyday people who come to know who they are, who begin to recognize their story, their future. They are ordinary people who know that they are not anonymous. Jesus calls each one of us by name. Day by day, He gives us new gifts, new energy. Jesus is not just present on the altar, in the tabernacle. Jesus lives in each of us.

St. Teresa of Avila had a wonderful experience of knowing that the Trinity — Father, Son, and Holy Spirit — were within her as in a beautiful crystal mansion, in fact, seven different mansions. The deepest presence of God is already given to us. The Holy Spirit is given to us so that we can come to recognize who we are and the gifts we have already received.

Jesus said, "This day this Word is being fulfilled in your midst." At each Eucharist, each one of us affirms that this Word, that this mission, this gift, this call is being made visible. We are the body and blood of Christ. Every one of us is important and significant. We cannot exist without one another. We cannot become who we are called to become without each other.

We are not only united with one another in Christ, we are bonded with the company of heaven. Every patron saint can easily become just another name, can become so familiar that we cease to acknowledge the gifts they have to share, or, the saint can become a member of the family. It is so easy to forget the communion of Saints, that those who are with Christ are not dead. They are alive. They are always doing something. They have been given a power by God to share with us. What do our patron saints tell us about ourselves? as individuals? as a Church? What difference does a name make? What difference does a saint make? So often a prophecy lives in a name whether it be our own name, the name of our parish, the name by which we choose to be called.

Jesus found His place in Scripture. He found His place in the plan of God. He said His "Yes." We are always at a new beginning in our lives. We are always being invited to find our place in the plan of God, in the Word already written. Every one of us has a place. Every one of us is given a new name. God is always pouring His Spirit into us. So we begin our lives anew with the Gospel of joy. "And the joy of the Lord must be your strength" (Ne 8:10).

All the members are important, because only together can we be the body of Christ. We are all called to come and stand in the midst of our community and dare to claim who we are. "Behold, I make all things new" (Rv 21:5). Jesus is doing something wonderful in our midst. The saints in their communion with us have a special bond with us. We need only to claim the grace that each of our patrons gives to us. We are called to rediscover their strength in our powerlessness, their holiness and their "Yes." We are called to become like little children. We are called each day to fulfill God's word, to fulfill God's hope, to fulfill God's invitation, to become the fullness of all God wants us to be. We are invited to say our, "Yes, I am the body of Christ." "Yes, I am the blood of Christ." "Yes, I know my place in the Word of God and plan to live it!"

I Believe in God, I Just Never Thought He Existed!

> The final command of Jesus as He ascended into heaven: "Go forth to all nations, making disciples of all people, and baptize them in the name of the Father and of the Son and of the Holy Spirit." (Mt 28:19)

Did your baptism take? Do you remember your baptism? Is it alive in you? Is it a well springing up to life everlasting? Did you act out of your baptism this past week? To what and to whom did you give your primary time?

I wonder about the man who had the courage to ask Jesus what is the greatest of the commandments. There are 613 commandments in the Torah. I wonder how long he wrestled with how he was to live his life. Perhaps he was overwhelmed with the 613 and wanted to find out from Jesus which was the most important one, which should he really live? What did you think about this week? What would you say is the focus, the "commandment" of your life? To what do you give your mind and your heart, your being, your body? What absorbs your energy, your attention? How important is God? How important is your neighbor? Take time to sit down and reflect, to what do you give your time? to what do you give your heart? to what do you give your mind? Do you ever wonder about God? When did you pray this week? Are you in any way fascinated by God? Do you ever wake up in the middle of the night and wonder what it's all about, what's happening to you, to your life, where you are going, how you are doing? We can take our cars to a garage to be hooked to a computer scan to find out what's happening or not happening within our car. But do we ever take the time to look at what is happening in us? You are a good person, otherwise you wouldn't be concerned about your spiritual growth, but do you allow the Word of God to, in any way, influence you?

What did you do this week out of your faith? How is Jesus decisive in your life? Did He make any difference? Does your faith make any difference in the way you live your life? Or is it on "automatic pilot"? In the film, *Oh, God!* John Denver begins to have extraordinary experiences of God in his life. His wife, who goes to church every Sunday (he didn't), couldn't believe any of it. Failing to explain it to her, he confronted her one day with, "I thought you were the believer in this family!" After all, she went to church every Sunday. She was a good woman. But she replied, "Well, I *believe* in God, I just never thought He *existed.*" I never thought He could come into my life and make a difference.

From what do you derive the greatest joy in your life? What is the meaning of your life? It's so easy *not* to think. It's so easy *not* to pray. It's so easy *not* to believe. It's so easy to make the minimal the maximal of our life: Going to church on Sunday is the minimum, it's not the maximum. "Keep holy the Lord's day." "Love the Lord, your God, with your whole heart, with your whole mind and soul, with your whole being." When you hear that, do you feel like crawling under the pew? Is that a judgment? How much time, how much energy, how much devotion do you give to the Lord, your God? Or, do you have a God? What or who makes a difference in your life? We need an examination of conscience again and again.

When was the last time you made Sunday holy? When was the last time you tried to make a visit to the church? When was the last time you prayed the rosary with your family? Do you take time each day to think of those special events and mysteries of Our

Lord's life and how they touch your life? When was the last time you prayed in your family? Do you have a Bible? Do you keep it on the television so you can look at it once in a while during the commercial breaks? Or should you keep it on top of the refrigerator where you can't miss it? Have you ever read the life of a saint? Who are your heroes? How many hours do we spend watching television? How good it would be to get in touch with our family tree, the people who can in some way energize us and help us discover who we are!

Who is your God? Not by saying, "Yes, yes," or "Lord, Lord," or "Father, Father," or coming to Mass on Sunday will you be complete. Is that what your life is all about?

With what are you fascinated? The greatest joy we can ever experience is the experience of God, Father, Son, and Holy Spirit. Do you ever read the psalms and find the language to express what is within you? Do you hunger and thirst for the living God? Do you want to see God? Do you want to know Him? Is your baptism still alive? Baptism is the sign of the Father, Son, and Holy Spirit being poured into us. A great magnetic force awakens and we are drawn to God. It takes the whole community to make this life credible.

What will become of the newly baptized infant? What difference will this baptism make in her life, in the life of her parents, her grandparents, her great grandparents? Baptism is not just a ceremony. It is bigger than lightning and thunder and nuclear power. We believe that the Father, Son, and Holy Spirit descend upon the little child and she will never be the same again.

We believe the Trinity has descended upon us and that we will never be the same again. We are invited to renew our baptism, to stir up that indwelling reality of Father, Son, and Holy Spirit, to hear our call to be a holy person, so holy that we can't keep that reality within ourselves, that we are compelled to share it with others, that we become a world people. We are called and we are sent to make disciples of all nations, to baptize in the name of the Father, and of the Son, and of the Holy Spirit. We receive an immense capacity to love the Lord, our God, and our neighbor with our whole heart and with our whole soul, with our whole being.

Jesus came to cast fire upon the earth. We have done a good job of smothering it, of not recognizing it, of preventing our tremendous energy from changing the world.

Listen. Open your eyes and ears. Recognize what happened to you so long ago. Ask that the water of baptism might churn up within you. Ask that you might begin to let the Lord, your God, be God. Ask that you might recognize who you are and who you are called to become.

Get Into the Wheelbarrow

Where did your ashes go? As the weeks of Lent pass by, has there been any change? Do you have a sense of sacred time and sacred place? Are you happy to get into this joyful season? I asked four or five people in the sacristy, "How's your lent going?" Three of them said, "Good." One said, "Not bad." The other, "It's coming." How is your Lent? What is happening?

I was with some Methodist ministers recently and one of them told me a wonderful story that I want to share with you. It's the story of an aerialist who was able to walk a wheelbarrow across a high-wire. An American millionaire saw him in Europe and followed him for a while. He watched the aerialist go from hill to hill, from tall building to tall building. Finally the American approached him, "You must come to the States and do this over Niagara Falls. I'll pay for it." The aerialist asked, "Do you believe I can do it?" The American answered, "I believe you can." Somehow they strung that wire across Niagara Falls. The aerialist got his wheelbarrow on the wire and he walked across the whole of Niagara Falls. Then he turned around and wheeled that wheelbarrow all the way back. When he came down, he asked the American, "Do you believe I can do it?" "Do I believe you can do it?! I saw you!" "Yes," he said, "but do you really, really believe I can do it?" He answered, "Yes." And the aerialist responded, "Get in the wheelbarrow!"

Are you really a disciple of Jesus? Are you really, really a disciple of Jesus? Will you get in the wheelbarrow? Will you get in the boat? What evidence is there that you believe?

Do you know how far back you go? The life that you carry within you, how long has it been passed on to you? Do you know that you carry within you the blood of Noah? You were in the ark. All of us were. All life comes from life, and Noah became the source of a new beginning after the flood. There's something of each one of us there with Noah. God has made a covenant with us. There is a rainbow in us — not just on certain days. There is a rainbow within us because God has made a covenant, a covenant of friendship with each one of us.

Are you led by the Spirit? How has the Spirit led you so far this week?

Are you good? Are you really *good*? Not "good at what?", but are you "good"? Do you experience your own goodness? Are you good at work? Are you good at prayer? Are you good at relationships? Are you good at friendship? What's the nicest thing anyone has ever said about you? What are you good for? What are you good with? Do you have a good spirit? Do you have a spirituality? Augustine once said, "The one who sings well, prays twice." I've often wondered why it hasn't been said that, "The one who works well, prays twice"? Does prayer make a difference in your work?

There was a wonderful, religious community that originated in England in 1747 and emigrated to America shortly thereafter. The community became known as the "Shakers." They held that whatever they did, they did personally for God. Their furniture is considered the finest furniture ever made in America, very expensive today. — They did such fine work!

How "good" is your family? Are you good at being "family"? Are you good at being able to be with each other? Are you good at forgiving? Are you good at loving? We pray that through His Spirit we may come to recognize our hidden self. Jesus prayed and He fasted. What do you fast from? Why do you fast? We fast because we are addictive, we are compulsive, we get into bad habits. We need to rediscover our freedom. We fast in order to be free, to resist being compulsive. We fast in order that we might have some time. What is your fast? We fast in order that we can pray, that we can be really present to ourselves.

You know, once upon a time, people worked in order that they could have more time to simply "be" who they are, and to be with those they cared about. Now, somehow, we've got the whole thing turned upside down. We rest in order that we can work more and more and more. The Aborigines in Australia provide for all their needs in twelve hours a week, and the rest of their time they spend to celebrate life, to enjoy themselves, and to enjoy one another. What's the average time required to provide the needs of this community? Minimally forty, sixty, eighty hours a week. When's the last time you had a Sabbath, when you could claim a whole hour for yourself, or a half day, in order to experience your own goodness, your own life, to experience joy?

Some twenty years ago, I went into a desert. I spent a month in the Sahara Desert. It was the finest experience of my life. I had nothing to do except read the Scripture and live the rhythm of nature. No electricity, running water, meat, vegetables, fruit. I lived on dates, rice, canned sardines and some moldy bread: I lost a pound a day for thirty days. But I was never hungry. It was so good to have so much time. To live with a sense of God all day. To know that my life is limited. Very few will ever have that luxury.

The most important moment came the last day I was in the Sahara. I was coming to experience that I carried a hermitage within myself and I no longer needed to stay in the desert. Each of us has our own desert within our self. There are wild demons within us and there are angels, but there is so much goodness.

We pray and we fast in order that we can come to love. There's only one sadness in life: that is to not be a whole person, to not be who we were made to be, to not be holy, to not learn to bear the beams of love, to not be that love to others. The season of Lent is that time to discover our goodness, to discover our grace, to discover our power to love. How important this time is! How important it is for us to fast and to pray and to come to discover our own goodness.

I was giving a retreat recently when a mother came to share with me the story of her son. He is autistic, so deep within himself that he cannot speak. But his mother has learned to help him communicate by the pressure she has upon his hand, and by this pressure she types for him. He's eleven years old. This is one of his reflections:

> If I could give the world a gift, I give it peace to make people free. Federal gentlemen arbitrate treaties green with concepts given them by God. Every decision gets less generous than before. If friends elect tumultuous proclamations of violence every time they relate to humankind, man-made feelings justify great law. Peace takes great feelings of genuine love. Feel, generous people. Benefit friends around the globe with gentleness. Great gifts come in small moments of silence, and every person must listen for their gift.
>
> — An eleven year old, autistic prophet!

Can I Forgive Someone for Not Being Holy?

Karl Menninger, the great American psychologist from Topeka, Kansas, wrote a book several years ago entitled *Whatever Happened to Sin?* Do you ever wonder about that: whatever happened to sin? I'm tempted to stand at the door following the liturgy and ask each one, "When was your last confession?" The other door would probably be jammed. I'm sure many would respond, "What business is it of yours?" or take the fifth amendment. Consider the last time you felt a need for forgiveness, the last time you forgave someone.

Whatever has happened to sin? What has happened to the Sacrament of Reconciliation? Over the past few years, I haven't heard confessions at the parish very often, but from the few times I have I would estimate that about 25 of the 4,000 in that parish celebrate the Sacrament of Reconciliation each month.

Some of you elders may remember the parish of your youth, when people would line up around the entire church waiting for confession. Do you remember that? Priests were kept busy in the confessional all Saturday afternoon, sometimes all Saturday morning and evening. I remember a priest who used to be an associate at St. Peter's in Harper Woods, my first parish. He had a little counter and he counted eleven hundred confessions at Christmas time one season. Eleven hundred confessions! I wish I were kept busy in the Sacrament of Reconciliation three days a week! There doesn't seem to be much of a demand.

Isn't it wonderful we've gotten beyond sin? That we no longer need reconciliation? What a poverty we have fallen into! Perhaps this accounts for the violence of our society, that we can't keep up building enough prisons.

What an incredible historical week it was when Israel and the P.L.O. committed themselves to seek the way of peace together. I spent four months in the Holy Land at the beginning of that year. I was overwhelmed with the level of violence and hatred. I was absolutely convinced that never in our day could they ever forgive what they had done to one another. That there was no peace ever possible. But, though the process is still far from finished as we enter the new millennium, it seems I may have been wrong. Something they began in December 1992 — perhaps around the Feast of the Immaculate Conception — resulted in papers signed on the Birthday of Our Lady, the eighth of September 1993, only five months after my visit. The risen Christ is still in our world. Peace is not human, it is divine. Whenever forgiveness and reconciliation happen we know God is present.

We are all trained and conditioned in "justice," an eye for an eye, a tooth for a tooth. We have learned it well. We say there's "no fault," but we keep high insurance premiums. We don't have that much to forgive. Not many of us have seen wives raped, children shot, nor been beaten almost to death. Few of us have much to forgive in terms of what the rest of the world has experienced. But when we see the incredible happenings of recent memory: the Israelis and Palestinians committing themselves to peace, the collapse of the Berlin Wall, the resolution of countless disputes in South Africa, Uganda, and Nigeria, the attempts to bring lasting peace to Bosnia, Kosovo and Serbia, we recognize that the risen Christ is still working. How much more are we called to reconciliation and forgiveness! How do you know you are forgiven? It's not only by going to confession. Confession of sins is not enough, but if we don't confess our sins and promise to amend our life, then we do not have the capacity to forgive. Pope John Paul II lamented that one of the greatest poverties of our time is our incapacity to experience the joy of forgiveness, the joy of reconciliation.

What were your sins this week? Did you get angry? Whom did you talk about? With whom were you frustrated? How many times did you have to forgive someone? What's the level of joy in your heart this morning because you have forgiven? How many times each day we need to forgive someone for something! To be forgiven ourselves! How many of your brothers and sisters are you no longer connected with because something happened a long time ago — so long ago that you can't even remember what or why, only that you know you're not talking to her/him any more? What's the most difficult thing you've had to forgive? Infidelity? Divorce? A child disappointing you? How many people stay away on Sunday morning because they cannot forgive the Church? or some law? some priest? some sister? some bishop? In recent years, we have all been hurt and scandalized by the sins of some whom we once held in very high esteem. Did you ever think you'd have to forgive a priest, a bishop, a president for scandal, for their sin?

What does it mean to forgive? What does it mean to love? Someone once told me that, "To forgive is to love someone for not being holy, for not being a saint, for not being whom you needed or wanted that person to be." If forgiveness ever happens in us, then it means we are no longer living out of ourselves. To sin, to err is human as Shakespeare said, but to forgive is divine. How do we let the divine come into us? How do we forgive? It's not with words. Forgiveness is not enough. How do we heal? How do we continue to be present to those who have done violence to us, who have destroyed us? How can enemies ever negotiate with one another? How can we negotiate with certain members of our family, with certain friends who are no longer friends? How do you forgive someone who has betrayed you? How do we get forgiveness? "We all destroy the one we love — the coward with a kiss, the brave one with a sword." (Oscar Wilde)

How do we admit who we are, claim our identity? Two men

went up to the Temple to pray: one bragged about the wonderful things he did that week, the other would not even lift his head but stayed in the back and cried out, "Lord, be merciful to me, a sinner." There is something very holy in recognizing one's sin, in recognizing that when we are forgiven, then we are changed. Each one of us is called to "be," and to allow Christ to be in us. At the Consecration, we hear again and again the words of every liturgy, "This is the cup of My Blood, the Blood of the new and everlasting covenant. It will be shed for you and for all so that sins may be forgiven. Do this in memory of Me." Our deepest religious act is not prayer. It is forgiveness. What is unique about the Catholic faith is to claim and believe in the forgiveness of sins, not just by the priest, but that every one of us is empowered to forgive one another for what we have done to each other.

How often are you in need of forgiveness? Peter asked, "Lord, how many times shall we forgive?" The Jewish traditions hold that "God can forgive any sin committed against Himself, but He cannot forgive what you have done to one another. You must go and be reconciled." Jesus says, "When you come to the altar and there remember that you have sinned against someone, leave your gift at the altar. Go and first be reconciled." If we acted upon that, would not the church be emptied?

Can I forgive? Can I forgive myself? Can I forgive my brother, my sister, my friend? Can I forgive someone for not being holy?

UNTIL I CAN SWALLOW THEM

One of the most significant Scripture passages in terms of our identity as Catholics is the sixth chapter of St. John's Gospel, sixty-six incredible and awesome verses that include Jesus' feeding a vast crowd of about 5,000 with five barley loaves and two dried fish. Sometimes because we have heard the story, our story, so often, we forget. We forget what it is all about. We forget who we are. We forget who we are called to become. Is this multiplication of material food not but a foretaste of our Eucharist? Eucharist, *eu charis* or charity, means gift and grace.

This event in the life of Jesus was akin to the Passover Feast. Jesus is the Lamb of God, saving His people by leading them through the desert. Here the people followed Jesus. Where do you find yourself in this particular Gospel passage? one of the crowd? one of the disciples? the child with bread and fish? Every time we hear the Word of God, we know it is autobiographical. The Good News is our story. It is not just representative of times past. It is today. Now.

The people followed Jesus because through Him were revealed wonderful signs of God's grace: raising people from the dead, giving eyesight to the blind, healing paralytics, lepers and others from all manner of illness. Perhaps they came for themselves, perhaps they brought friends or members of their family with them, perhaps they came out of curiosity. Whatever their motive, Jesus' concern was to feed them, to assure they would not go away hungry. He wanted them to have something to eat.

Ever ready to offer the disciples opportunities to see, to understand, and to act, Jesus asked them, "Where shall we buy bread for these people to eat?" The disciples were not yet prepared and answered much as we would probably respond today, "We cannot do it." Each time we hear this story, Jesus is offering us a new opportunity to see, to understand, and to act. Just as Jesus taught the disciples to pray, "Give us this day, our daily bread," so we are invited to ask for this blessing and to expect God's grace to bless us. What was your bread this week? How did Jesus feed you? How did our Lord nourish you? How have you responded to all you have received? Every time two or three are gathered together in Christ's name, there is something to celebrate, something to thank God for, something to ask of God.

Imagine these people two thousand years ago. Living as they did in desert country, it is unlikely that they would travel even for a day without taking some kind of nourishment with them. So much can be said about the mystery of the loaves and fish. Perhaps the miracle was not so much that Jesus multiplied five barley loaves and two dried fish in an extraordinary way, so that everyone was filled and there were twelve baskets remaining. Perhaps more astonishing was the miracle of five thousand individuals sharing and eating in communion with one another. Would it not be a far greater miracle that people would share what they had with one another? Far greater than creating food, as the devil had tempted Jesus to do in the desert. Is that not one of the greatest temptations of our material life: wanting something for nothing rather than sharing what we already have?

The people followed Jesus. We continue to follow Jesus. We are drawn to the daily bread of Eucharist. We come to be renewed, to be nourished by the Word of God. The Word came down from heaven and became one of us. The Word continues to live with us in the form of bread and wine, in the lives of one another. Each time we come to the table, we pray, "come unity" — community, with one another. This is the whole point. Jesus touches each one of us helping us to understand that because we are His body and blood, we are the body and blood of one another. The grace and gift of Eucharist is that we become one. There is one body, there is one Lord, there is one body over all, with all and in all.

To come to the Eucharist is not simply to believe in Jesus or pray to God. We come to be with and to see one another. Eucharist is so incredible! When we receive Jesus, who are we receiving? What are we receiving under the form of bread and wine? We are receiving the whole body of Christ! Jesus is always identifying Himself with us. Remember Paul's experience on the road to Damascus. He said, "Who are you?" The response was, "I am Jesus, whom you are persecuting." We are drawn to Eucharist to come closer to one another that Jesus might get closer to us.

Do you know that expression, "I can't swallow that," "I can't swallow him," "I can't swallow her"? Do you realize what that means? It means that I can't accept, I can't take that idea or person into myself, I can't own it as my own. If we cannot swallow our brother or sister, it also means that we cannot swallow Christ. He claims each one of us, and each one belongs to Him and to one another. Every time we come to receive the Body and Blood of Christ, we are called to be one with Him. We are called to a state of grace, a state of friendship. Otherwise, how could we receive Him? With each communion, Christ expands our capacity to receive one another, to come closer to one another, to belong to one another. In each Eucharist something of Jesus is deposited in us to be passed on as a blessing to others.

When the priest pronounces the words of consecration over the bread and wine, they are Jesus' words as a sign of what is to happen in us. If only the bread and wine were changed, then nothing would really happen to us. Eucharist is meant to change us. When we come to receive the Body and Blood of Christ, it is presented to us with the words, "Body of Christ," "Blood of Christ." When we respond, "Amen," we are really saying, "Yes. Yes I am the body of Christ. Yes I am the blood of Christ. Yes we are the Body and Blood of Christ."

What is it that brings us together day after day, week after week? Jesus. Jesus draws us. We are always being broken. We are always being estranged. We are always being discovered. Only Jesus can draw us to Himself and to one another. The great gift of Jesus is that He so loved each one of us, He put His mark upon us. He died that each one of us might know life abundantly. If we could only recognize who we are! "If you but knew the gift of God and who it is who lives in you!," who lives in your next door neighbor, who lives in the persons you were sent to this week! Our whole identity with God is rooted in Jesus who dwells in our souls. God is that close to us!

Most of us have read something of the lives of the great saints. A neighbor of mine many years ago told me of the night he stopped by the old Capuchin Monastery in Detroit. Fr. Solanus Casey (now being considered for sainthood) was praying. Fr. Solanus' prayer was so intense, his love so deep, that he was actually lifted off the ground. This has happened to a number of the saints. Have you ever been lifted off the ground in prayer? That is a *little* mystical experience. The *greater* mystical experience is that Jesus comes and lives in us. He cries out, "Let me live in you!" He keeps on saying, "Come, come, come. Listen, listen, listen. Eat. Drink."

How can we ever forget that we carry Jesus in ourselves? We carry Him not for ourselves alone, we are to be Christ's gift for others. We are called to evangelize, to be the bread of life, the Word of life. We are called to recognize Christ in our brothers and sisters, to live no longer for ourselves. If we but knew who it is that hungers for us!

The sign that we truly receive Eucharist is that we come closer to one another. Jesus' presence overflows from us into the lives of others. Paul echoes Jesus' invitation: "...live a life worthy of the calling you have received, with perfect humility, meekness, and patience, bearing with one another lovingly" (Eph 4:1-2). Live a life worthy of the Eucharist you receive. "Make every effort to preserve the unity which has the Spirit as its origin and peace as its binding force" (Eph 4:3). There is but one body. We are the body of Christ. Jesus lives in us and has given to each one of us a charism, a gift.

As we consider Jesus taking those five loaves and two fish from the young lad, we wonder who he was. We cannot help but admire His extraordinary generosity. What a beautiful experience to see someone who is generous. Some gifts can be very selfish, some adults are very selfish. At times, we are all selfish. But every once in a while we witness a moment of great generosity. Imagine the joy of that little boy coming forth to offer all he had. Imagine his joy when, after everyone had been filled, twelve baskets full remained. To whom do you think Jesus gave those twelve baskets?

Love is never enough until you pass it around, until you give it away. We have been given so much. Jesus is always here ready to take us, receive us; Jesus is always here to bless us; Jesus is always here to break us from ourselves, to free us from ourselves, and then to pass us around.

We are already in the heart of Jesus. It is good to stop now and then, to really stop, to take time, to contemplate, and to look at who we are. Look at who the person next door is. Look at what Jesus is doing in us. Let us pray to become as that little child, willing to give all we have so that Jesus can take us, bless us, break us, and pass us around so that the world around us may be transformed through His love and mercy in us!

So let us say our yes, "Yes, I am the body of Christ." Then, let us say a second yes, "Yes, you are the body of Christ." When others begin to recognize Christ by seeing how we love one another, they, too, will be drawn to the table saying, "Yes, they are the body of Christ, the joy and hope of others." Happy are those who hear Jesus calling and who dare to risk loving one another, those who have the courage to become generous. Jesus is always waiting to come, waiting to make His home in us. Who will invite Him in?

Celebrate Yourself!

Little Point of Nothingness

Waiting, seeking, anticipating: these are all common states of all humankind. Every one waits. We all wait for something, for someone. What are you waiting for? Who or what are you searching for? How much of your ordinary day is spent in waiting, in anticipating, in searching?

One of the great "seekers" in the Gospel is the woman at the well. The Samaritan woman who waited for "something" to happen or for "someone" to come to her at the well one noon. Do you envy her in some way? What an incredible moment she experienced! This Samaritan woman was a woman who was different from the others. The women of that time went out early in the morning, always together. A "good" woman never went to the well at noon time, and never alone because that was the time when the men might be going by. So if she was there, she was looking for something: excitement, business, perhaps. Looking. Waiting. Anticipating. Imagine her going out to the well on this particular day and finding Jesus waiting for her. This is no accident. Perhaps all her life she had been looking without knowing exactly what she sought. Always looking for something, someone.

What do we know of her? She was a Samaritan. She had already gone through five husbands; the man she was living with now, her sixth, was not her husband. Imagine her choosing Jesus for her seventh seduction! From relationship to relationship, she had continued to look. No one, no man had satisfied her. What must have been that moment when she met Jesus, who had been waiting for her all her life — that moment when she realized she had been looking for Jesus all her life?

The Gospel is not simply a history book. The Gospel is a mirror. The Gospel is about us. Every time we hear the Gospel, we should ask "When is this going to happen to me?" Jesus has been waiting for each of us all of our life. Even if we're not aware of it, we have been looking for Him all of our life. We never know when and where that rendezvous is going to take place. Where is Jesus waiting for you? Where is He waiting today? Where will you find Him?

The Samaritan woman had not gone to the synagogue to look. She remained in the sphere of her everyday life, her everyday business. What would be the parallel of that today? Would it be a bar? Do you ever imagine Jesus waiting for you in a bar and asking you, "Will you buy me a drink?" Or it could be a shopping mall, a gas station. Anytime you meet people — anyone you meet — could be Jesus. What will happen? Are you ready for that meeting? Do you expect it? Do you anticipate that something wonderful and unexpected will happen to you? Are you ready?

It was Jesus who initiated the dialogue at the well. The woman was suspicious — perhaps pleased. The two were all alone. Then Jesus said, "Give me a drink." When she started her dialogue, Jesus turned the conversation all around and said, "If you but knew the gift of God and who it is that is speaking to you, that is with you...."

Some thirty years ago, a parishioner asked me what my favorite words of Scripture were. I immediately responded with these very words of the Gospel: "If you but knew the gift of God...." If you but knew the gift of yourself. If you but knew the gift of one another.

I came across a wonderful reflection of Thomas Merton in his book, *Conjectures of a Guilty By-Stander*:

> At the center of our being is a point of nothingness which is untouched by sin and by illusion, a point of pure truth, a point

> or spark which belongs entirely to God, which is never at our disposal, from which God disposes of our lives, which is inaccessible to the fantasies of our mind or the brutalities of our own will.

"At the center of our being is a point of nothingness which ... belongs entirely to God...." Do you ever get in touch with your own innocence, with your own capacity for God?

Do you ever take a deeper look at where you are and where you are going. We are all called to remain open to the deep realities within ourselves.

Merton goes on to say:

> This little point of nothingness and of absolute poverty is the pure glory of God in us. It is so to speak His name written in us as our poverty, as our indigence, as our dependence, as our sonship and daughtership. It is like a pure diamond, blazing with the invisible light of heaven. It is in everybody, and if we could see it we would see these billions of points of light coming together in the face and blaze of a sun that would make all the darkness and cruelty of life vanish completely.... I have no program for this seeing. It is only given. But the gate of heaven is everywhere.

"If you but knew the gift of God...." If you could only experience in some way your capacity for God Himself, and to know that He is waiting. Where does He wait for you this week? Are you in some way on edge and waiting? Where will you wait for Him?

Do you ever allow yourself to be startled that you have a God? a God who knows you by name and is everywhere in your life? We cannot get out of Him. We are made of Him. At one moment, we were nothing and then He said a *word.* As He said to this woman, "I'll give you water that will well up into life everlasting." Paul tells us that this is not ordinary water, not that which we ordinarily drink. It is the love of God poured into our hearts. Imagine water that flows like love. As life has been breathed into us, so love is breathed into us. So is faith, and so is the capacity to love others. These are always happening, but we so rarely see.

Each of us is a disciple, and in some way we know a mystery, a sacrament, a hunger, a capacity. In some way, you know Jesus is waiting for you right now, right where you are. This is the well. In each of us there is a well, and somehow you were drawn to the well where Jesus has been waiting for you.

So easily we touch into our pockets of pain and the crosses that we do not choose, but there are also immense pockets of joy. In every Eucharist, Jesus creates a new pocket of joy, a new reservoir that is intended to be poured into us so that we live our life at a different level of consciousness, a new level of possibility, because we are never alone.

Jesus has drawn you. He's been waiting for you all of your life and He wants to pour Himself into you. "If you but knew the gift of God...." If you but knew the gift of yourself. If you but knew the gift of each person. If you could see the glory of God, His presence, His waiting. If we could only believe the truth. "I will give you that water of life. I will give you that love that it may be poured into you and overflow into the life of each person to whom I send you this week." Dare to believe that Jesus is waiting for you. Recognize how much in you is waiting for Him.

Greater than the Desert Person

> Repent, for the kingdom of Heaven is close at hand. (Mt 3:2)
>
> "This was the witness of John, when the Jews sent to him priests and Levites from Jerusalem to ask him, "Who are you?" he declared, he did not deny but declared, "I am not the Christ"... "Then who are you? We must take back an answer to those who sent us. What have you to say about yourself?" So he said, "I am, as Isaiah prophesied: a voice of one who cries in the desert: Prepare a way for the Lord. Make His paths straight." (cf. Jn 1:10-23)

Who is John the Baptist? The Gospel is never just a history lesson, something that happened two thousand years ago. Who does the Word of God come to? Who are the John the Baptists in today's world? Do you know your identity? Every one of us is called to be John the Baptist because we have heard the Word of God. We respond to the Word as it touches us. The Gospel is the story for the people whose name the world does not know.

Who was this John the Baptist? The only child of a couple beyond the age of childbearing, John was a man in the desert. His parents may have died before he became a teenager. The description of John in the Scriptures is of a kind of wild man and a rebel. He wore strange clothes and he ate strange food. He had little patience with the Pharisees and Sadducees, using violent language and threatening them about the coming days. John would never have won a popularity contest! He was probably a member of one of the desert communities, a man with a single-focused purpose. John must have felt haunted by an urgent, inner voice all of his life.

And what has haunted us all of our lives? What is our quest throughout our lives? How often we ask, "Who am I?" "What is my life all about?" "Why did God create me?" We wait our whole life. Our life is an advent, a waiting and a longing to come to know who we are, what our life work is all about. Whether we put it into words or not, we are always yearning for God, for God to touch us, to use us and to send us forth.

In the desert, John waited for most of his life. He had an extraordinary experience in the womb of his mother, Elizabeth. A cousin of his mother named Mary came to visit. When Mary came close to Elizabeth, John leaped in her womb for joy. John experienced the joy of recognition of the Christ, the Awaited One, right in his mother's womb. That joy never left him.

Each one of us has been touched within our mother's womb. Before our birth each of us was called to be holy. We were called to be a presence of Christ. I am sure that John never forgot that joy, just as we never really forget our baptism. Something special has happened to each of us. Every one of us is wonderfully and significantly important — even though we may not realize that ourselves. Each one of us is loved, touched and called by God.

Year after year, John prayed and struggled in the desert, perhaps not even quite knowing himself who he was or what his life was all about. A strange man. A faith-filled man. Yet one day, he knew that God had touched him in a new way, that God had called him forth for a special purpose. So, he went along the Jordan River proclaiming that something very wonderful was about to happen.

The people were called to repent, to turn around and to change their minds and their hearts. People came to him from Jerusalem and all of Judea and the whole Jordan district. As they went up to be baptized, they confessed their sins and made a new beginning. No matter what their life had been, they repented of their sins. John understood then that he had been called by God to proclaim something new, to proclaim that someone greater than he was to come. John was the proclaiming evangelizer; Mary was the hidden and silent evangelizer without any words. As John proclaimed to every person he met, he opened their heart. What a power he must have had! Fulfilling the prophecy of Isaiah, the power of the Most High spoke through him. John became the voice in the desert crying, "Make ready a way for God. Clear the Lord a straight path."

Something of John the Baptist lives in us by the power of our baptism, our confirmation and every Eucharist. In fact, Jesus said that the least in the kingdom of heaven is GREATER even than John. Jesus said that John was the greatest man born of woman, that he was greater than Abraham, Moses, and David of the Old Testament. The greatest of anyone who had been born of woman. Yet, the least of the kingdom of heaven is greater than John.

Do you know who you are? Do you know the power that is at work in you? Each one of us has an incredible power, more than anything we can ask or imagine. The Lord is waiting for us, for each one of us.

Many churches today are small, like mustard seeds. Each one is a voice crying in the wilderness, crying out for justice in an unjust and violent world, crying out for peace in a world torn by war, crying out for freedom where there is oppression, crying out for the Word to be heard, crying out for individuals, institutions, countries to repent and to know the joy of the Lord. Every community of prayer, every community of risk, every community of outreach is that voice. Each individual is called today to pray, to pray fervently, to be the voice that will be heard in the wilderness of our cities, our countries, our world. Valleys must be filled and mountains must be made low, the winding way is to be made straight and the rough ways made smooth, so that all of humanity will see and know and live the salvation of the Lord.

Paul's prayer at the beginning of Philippians seems today like a voice crying in the wilderness. Imagine this prayer of Paul paraphrased as a prayer of Jesus over us in our day:

> I thank Abba whenever I think of you, and every time I pray for you all, I always pray with joy for your partnership in the Gospel from the very first day up to the present. You can be quite confident that I, who began a good work in you, will go on completing it until the day I come again. It is only right that I should feel like this toward you all, because you have a place in my heart, since you have all shared together in the grace that has been mine, both my sufferings and my work defending and establishing the Gospel. For Abba will testify to how much I long for you to come to me; and it is my prayer that your love for one another may grow more and more with the knowledge and complete understanding that will help you to come to true discernment, so that you will be innocent and free of any trace of guilt when I come, entirely filled with the fruits of uprightness through my love for you, for the glory and praise of our Father, Abba.

This is the Word of God. We are the voice God counts on to cry in the wilderness of today's world.

DAILY BREAD OF THE HEART

Each year we are invited to prepare ourselves for the great season of Lent. This special time is not just a period for our personal fasting, almsgiving, prayer, and renewal. We, as a world community, take upon ourselves the sin of the world and try to bring new life, a new creation, into the world. We need to take time to pray and to allow our world to speak to us in terms of what Christ is calling us to become, not just as individuals, but as a community of believers.

Jesus proclaimed Himself as a prophet. Sometimes we think of a prophet as someone who foretells the future. That is not Jesus' meaning of a prophet. When He speaks of Himself as a prophet, or speaks of any of the prophets of the Old Testament, He refers not to foretelling the future. Rather He regards prophets as those who were instruments of God, those through whom God could speak. Every one of us is someone through whom God can speak, simply because God made us. Each one of us is a word of God that He has not finished expressing. Each one of us is a mystery that is inexhaustible. Each of us is called to recognize God in us, God with us.

Jesus stood up in the midst of His people and announced what His mission, His life's work, was to be. He told them He was sent by God to heal, to forgive, to care, and to visit. We have all been given the gift of faith. We know that we live not only for ourselves, that we are called to live for others. We acknowledge that we cannot do this by ourselves. Yet, because Jesus lives in us and each day empowers us, inspires us, lives and breathes in us, we are enabled to be the good news for others. Because Jesus is our light and our salvation, whom shall we fear? What an incredible gift!

Paul's description of the mission of Jesus is so beautiful: the way that surpasses all others, which is simply to love. To more fully understand the impact of what love is as described in the thirteenth chapter of Corinthians, try this exercise. In place of the word "love," place your own name or use the first person pronoun "I." See and feel how this echoes in you. If I dare to say, "I am patient, I am kind, I am not jealous, I do not put on airs, I am not snobbish, I am never rude, I am not self-seeking, I am not prone to anger; neither do I brood over injuries, I do not rejoice in what is wrong, but I rejoice with the truth," how uncomfortable I feel. Yet, this *is* the way we are prophets, the way we are witnesses, the way we make visible who Jesus is.

None of us can claim to have this total, unconditional love, because this is not the love of the human heart. When Paul speaks about love, he is not speaking about friendship, of the love between man and woman, of the love of children and parents. He is speaking about a new kind of life, a new kind of presence, that only comes because Jesus lives within us. The only one who can claim to love so fully, so wholly, is Jesus Himself.

We are to draw Jesus into us. We do this through prayer. We know what prayer is, we know about contemplation, we need to take a long, loving look at reality, a long, loving look at what is most important. We need to take a long, loving look at Jesus. Often.

We have been given a mind that is hungry for truth, a mind that wants to absorb with understanding the wisdom of everything. What an amazing gift we have as a human person, that we have a mind capable of reaching out to the stars, of touching the whole universe! One of our early American writers, Ralph Waldo Emerson, jotted down in his notebook one day that "the sky is the daily bread of the eye." The sky, the universe, delights the human eye, the smallest of our sense organs. Yet, the eye can see the sun

93,000,000 miles away and billions of stars at night. How small our eye is! How much it can encompass! What our eyes see feeds our hunger for all truth.

We also have a heart. We not only want to absorb all of reality, but we want to be absorbed by other life. We are always hungry. We are always looking for more. The incredible truth is that we are becoming more, because what we hunger and search for is not just our creation, not just our imagination. We hunger and yearn for Jesus to come to us; we long to *know* that He is as close as our own heart, our own breath, our own blood. It is Jesus who makes us prophets, who gives us the capacity to love more, because He dwells in us.

Paul names a dozen different things that love is not. Only two things are the test of our love: our kindness and our patience. How easy it is to be kind and patient to someone we are just meeting for the first time, a stranger. The real test comes in our family, between our friends, not just in the big moments but in the little moments of everyday living. When it happens that we are kind and patient, then we know that something more than ourselves, someone more than ourselves, is there. We know the Lord is present. In those moments we know what love is.

As we prepare for the Lenten season, for our new springtime, let us pray for this kind of love, the overflow of Jesus in our lives. Let us ask for truth and wisdom. Let us dare to stand up in the midst of our community and be kind and patient, loving and truthful. Then we shall know that Jesus is with us and that His word, His dream, is being fulfilled in us and through us. Others will know we are Christians by our love for one another.

Continuous Conscious Communion

Jesus says to pray always. To pray is to be conscious, to be alive, to live life more abundantly. We are Christians, not simply because we believe in God. We are Christians because we claim to have Jesus' experience of the Father. Jesus' experience of the Father was, "I am never alone. The Father is always with me." What is your sense of the Divine Presence? How do you exercise and use your faith day by day? Do you believe that every day in some way He will touch your life? That every day He has a rendezvous with you? Jesus said to His disciples, "I'm going ahead of you into Galilee, and there I will meet you." Do you expect each day, in some way, that Jesus will manifest Himself to you? That's the act of hope. Like Zacchaeus climbing the sycamore tree to catch a glimpse of Jesus. Do you believe? Do you hope? Do you anticipate where Jesus will meet you today? It's kind of a miracle to get out of bed in the morning, isn't it? To wake up. To have the capacity to be. To know that you have feet to put into your shoes.

When you hear those words, "I am the Good Shepherd," it's not just a nice thought. You are not just hearing the 23rd Psalm which you hear, perhaps too often, at funerals. When Jesus says, "I am your Good Shepherd," do you allow something to stir within yourself? What is it like to have a good shepherd, to have someone who is always with you? Jesus says so extraordinarily, "My sheep know me as the Father knows me, and I know them and they hear my voice and they follow me." How did you hear His voice this week? What did you allow yourself to experience?

How does Jesus shepherd you? How does He allow you to breathe? We take for granted the air we breathe, unless there's something in the air. But we do nothing about the air. We do not create it. It's a total gift. The water we drink. The food we eat. Our capacity to breathe and to eat, to see, to touch, to taste. These are totally gifts. We are being shepherded by the Lord in every moment, every breath, every bite. How good it is for us to grow in that continuous conscious communion. To have a sense of His presence. To have a sense of everything in our life as gift. To grow in a spirit of gratitude. To grow in a sense of joy.

"Alleluia." It is a Hebrew word that means, "The Lord is here. Recognize Him. Praise Him. Celebrate Him." We can get used to the Word of God. It can become just a notion in our heads. How many "Alleluias!" did you say this week? Did you have any "alleluias"? It is the word of the fifty days of celebration of Easter. "Alleluia!" The Lord is here. Recognize Him. Celebrate Him. Thank Him. We are to be an alleluia people. We are to break out of ourselves.

When Jesus says, "I am the light of the world," He is very explicit in saying, "You are the light of the world." Every one of Jesus' "I am's," His identity, is a mirror of what our identity is to be. We do not yet know what we are to become. We do know our past, we can remember that. But it is important to anticipate, to look forward to, what we are becoming. We're never stuck in one place, there is something of us living and growing. We are becoming more than we could ever ask or imagine.

How and where do the words of Jesus find their reality in our lives? Every time we hear the Word of God, we should ask, "When did that happen this week?" "How did it happen?" "How am I changed because Jesus is my shepherd?" "I am never alone." "He's always doing something more, something beyond anything we could ever ask or imagine."

How do we let the truth of Jesus be our truth? How do we, each day, look for another moment of evidence that He loves us? Imagine someone who prays for you by name every day. Imagine someone who does some secret service for you, who loves you each day. Imagine someone who is always looking out for you, who assures you that you will never be alone — even as you walk through the valley of death.

Jesus does not prevent us from experiencing suffering. His Father did not prevent the cup from being given to Him. But the Father was with Him. And Jesus is with us. Each day we should look for that new grace to know that there is someone in our life, regardless how much "non-sense" is there. Jesus calls us to develop new eyes, new ears, a new heart. To know that Jesus is faithful to His promise that He is always shepherding us. He is always with us. He is always forgiving us. Always drawing us to new life. So many times during the day, we should cry out, "Thank You, Jesus. Thank You, Abba. Thank You, Holy Spirit. Alleluia!"

The Lord is here. Praise Him. Recognize Him. Celebrate Him. Share Him. Be joy filled. Be Easter people all year. Alleluia!

"WANTED" BY GOD

What is your favorite passage from the writings of St. Paul? He wrote half of the New Testament. It is very valuable for us to allow the Word of God to fill our minds and hearts. We get so much negative evangelization through the media. We have to counter bad news with the Good News. How good it is to be nourished by the words of Paul, the great witness of the resurrection, perhaps the one who most profoundly understood the mystery of Jesus.

My favorite of Paul's writing is the eighth chapter of his letter to the Romans. Is there a time when your faith runs thin, when you feel overwhelmed with all the things that are put upon you? Then, I assure you that lifting up and reading that eighth chapter of Romans will lift your heart. In Paul's words: "I am *absolutely convinced* that nothing in the past, or present, or yet to come, can ever separate us from the love of God in Christ Jesus, our Lord." *Nothing of the past or the present or what is yet to come can ever cut us off from the love of God!*

Do you have a sense of the Lord's presence with you? During this week, was there a moment when you could almost consciously and tangibly feel someone close to you? Not just God of the universe, but someone who knows you by name, someone who cares for you, someone who desires you and wants you.

Who is your God? So many of us have a negative image of God. For some, God is "the judge." For some God simply "is." How rarely do we allow ourselves to experience that we are loved by God. How rarely do we allow ourselves to recognize that God is love.

He can do nothing but love us. You are desired by God. You are wanted by God.

Imagine that you went to the post office and looked at the FBI's "wanted posters," but instead of the traditional faces, you saw your own picture and under it "Wanted By God." "Desired By God."

What is it to be "desired" by another person? What is it to be admired? Do you have a secret admirer? Someone who sends you gifts, flowers, a check, cash? Who wants you? Who needs you? Who loves you? Who will never leave you? Whom can you never lose? Your "self" and the Lord.

What makes our lives meaningful? That which enables us to be happy in spite of everything is to know that we are loved by someone, to know that we are desired by someone.

Imagine what Paul's experience must have been that he could say "I am *absolutely convinced* that nothing can ever separate me, that I can never lose God. That I can never lose His love for me personally and uniquely." What is it to be known and loved and desired by God? What is it to have an absolute conviction of God's love? In some way you do have a sense of God, otherwise there would be no sense reading these words. You do have a sense of the Lord's presence. It might be very remote. It might be very alive. It might be a sense of a loving companion presence. A sense of the Lord always in your life. Jesus wants us to experience that as concretely as that which we can see and taste and touch.

Many of the people I encounter each week are anonymous to me. I might recognize many faces, but I know few by name. That is frustrating. I wish I knew all by name. I know nothing about so many. So many know nothing about me. For most, I am anonymous. Many may know my face or my beard, but they do not know me. How much each of us needs someone in our life who knows us, who cares, who is concerned for us! We are drawn to pray for that.

The multitudes followed Jesus out into the desert. They spent the whole day with Him. Why? Why were they there? They were searching. They were looking. They were hungry. For Him. Something within each one of us searches, looks, hungers, prays. Something deep within each of us is always alive and always turning to God. We can't get rid of Him. Thank God we can't get rid of Him! God is always in our life, always inviting us to go further and deeper.

The disciples, seeing the hungry multitudes, came to our Lord and said, "Send the people away. We have nothing to feed them." But Jesus said, "They don't have to be sent away." To which they replied, "We have nothing except a few loaves and fish." (There was probably enough for the twelve of them, but for no one else. We usually find enough to take care of ourselves.) So they said "Send them away." But Jesus said "No." Give them something to eat — *yourself*."

How do you give yourself as nourishment? What do you have to give? The disciples thought they had nothing. Jesus always says, "Give me the little that you have." Then He takes, and He blesses, and He breaks, and He gives it away. Whether we are aware of it or not, He wants to take us and He wants to bless us and He wants to break us from all the things that prevent us from being given away. The Eucharist on the altar is a mirror of what is to happen to us. We may feel that we have nothing. He doesn't need much.

Recently I gave a retreat in Buffalo, New York. One night we went over to Niagara Falls. I've seen them a number of times, but this was the first time I had three hours just to look upon that million gallons a second that has been flowing for 12,000 years. Ten thousand years before Jesus was born, that Niagara River was going over those falls. I watched them from the top, then went down to the bottom and looked up at them. I realized that those magnificent falls, that tremendous volume of water, are nothing compared to the love that God has for each of us. A million gallons a second for 10,000 years before Jesus! It cannot compare to the kind of love, the kind of care, the kind of concern God has for each of us. Our Lord wants us to understand, He wants us to experience that love, and He wants to be a presence in our life, a presence we can never, never forget.

Jesus wants to be more deeply a loving companion presence in your life. So you respond. You are drawn. You are called to see and to touch and to feel. You are called to recognize that place deep within you that wants to be known and loved and desired. You are called to recognize that it is real. Jesus continues to give us something to eat — Himself. The sign that we understand, the sign that we receive, comes when we allow ourselves to be taken, blessed, broken, and given away.

Let us pray that we each dare to claim that "I am absolutely convinced that nothing in life or in death, the powers of this world or the other world, can ever separate us, cut us off, from the love of God in Christ Jesus our Lord."

Has Anyone Accused Your Family of Being Holy?

The Sunday after Christmas is always celebrated as the feast of the Holy Family. "Happy Feast Day!" Have you ever been accused of being a holy family? Does anyone call you a holy family? Years ago I was giving a course in marriage and I entitled it, "Marriage Is Holy." An old fellow came and asked, "Marriage is holy *what*?" You can fill in the blank.

The Church is very realistic. Ordinarily after Christmas we immediately celebrate the feast of St. Stephen, the first martyr. Thus, immediately after celebrating the birth of the child who was born to be a martyr, we celebrate the first Christian martyr, Stephen. In recent years, the Feast of the Holy Family and the Feast of St. Stephen have been combined. Perhaps this makes more sense than we realize. More than one theologian has said that the equivalent of martyrdom in the early Church is marriage and family life today. They were not joking, and there is something about marriage and family life today that calls for a kind of martyrdom, a kind of witness, a kind of faith, because never before has the family been more threatened.

How do you name your family? Do you ever call it a holy family? Perhaps this feast would be more appropriate for our time as the "suffering family." What family is not suffering?

Sometimes we have to unlearn the images we have of the holy family as a comfortable one-child family with no problems. We so easily forget that Mary and Joseph became refugees. Imagine their anguish that, because of their son, all the children born in that town around that time were massacred. It has continued to our day. The greatest victims of the world are little children. How many never even have a chance to breathe?

Mary and Joseph went into Egypt not knowing the language. They were refugees. They were a minority. Always hunted and oppressed. We know Mary probably was an early widow. We hear nothing of Joseph after the time Jesus was 12 years old in the Temple. Even going back to His own town, when Jesus began His public ministry, Jesus was not accepted in His home parish. They tried to kill Him. And when Jesus was almost killed in His own town, Mary became a woman of the roads. Her life was not easy. Most women's lives, most men's lives are not easy.

What is a holy family? What is a suffering family? What is an anxious family? All are wounded. Every child carries the wounds of the adults in their life. Every adult carries the wounds of his/her own childhood. Family life is not easy. As people of faith, you walk in the presence of God. You are never alone because Jesus and Mary and Joseph are part of your family.

How do you live that holiness? There are very few who believe enough in their own goodness. There are very few who believe in their own holiness. It's so important. One of my favorite books has been Salinger's book, *Frannie and Zoey*. One day Frannie said to Zoey, "I have a suspicion that there is a conspiracy to make me happy." Do you ever have that feeling — that there is a conspiracy to make you happy, to make you holy? Do you ever have a suspicion that your wife might be holy, or that your husband might be holy. Of course you know that it takes a martyr to live with a saint — and you never know which is which!

It's wonderful to have a suspicion of, or to catch a glimpse of, the holiness of your children. We have saints who had been recognized as saints since they were three years old. It is a wonderful thing to pray over your spouse, and once in a while to take a long loving look at the mystery of God, of Father, Son, and Holy Spirit, in them. We never recognize the depth of God's presence in each of us. We are rooted at the base of our being in God. We have come from God. Our whole life is a journey back to Him. He is with us all the way, inviting us to catch a glimpse of the holiness and the goodness of each person in our families.

We need to pray more. We don't recognize how secular we have become. How embarrassed we are with even the signs and symbols of God in our home! What is your family treasure? What have you invested most in? What are you going to hand down to your children? What are they going to do in remembrance of you? How many television sets have you bought? at $395 or $495? or personal computers? Do you ever think of buying an icon, a holy image of God that would be the center of your home, that would be handed down generation after generation? Is there any sign of who you are and what you've committed yourself to in your home? Do you have a holy corner? a sacred corner? Some people now display pictures of their parents and grandparents — a holy corner. That's wonderful. But have you prayed as a family? Did you pray yesterday aside from meals? Do you take time to read the word of God? Do you say a decade of the rosary? We used to say, "The family that prays together stays together." Claim the Feast of the Holy Family as your family day! Celebrate the holiness, the goodness, the generosity of your family. We haven't sufficiently taken church into our homes. We're far behind the Jewish community that celebrates the Shabbat Shalom every Friday night. And the Japanese always have a shrine to their ancestors, in the family home. How do we make our home sacred? How do we make it holy? We can't leave Jesus in the tabernacle. We are intended to take Him home and in some way to support our faith with tangible evidence.

How to be a holy family? How to have a sense of the sacred in your own home? Do you have an angel of your home? Angels are back "in." Have you ever thought of recognizing the angel of your own home? Are there moments of silence? (What am I talking about? What silence is there in any family?) Perhaps there are moments. Do you ever bless your children? Do you believe that you have been plunged into the priesthood of Christ? that every father and mother is to exercise their priesthood in their own home? Is there holy water in your own home? I never will forget my father blessing us with holy water every night when we got into bed. Do you ever bless your family? It doesn't have to be a solemn blessing, but just a little one-inch cross on their foreheads as they leave or come home. Do you believe in your own power to bless? The blessing is but a symbol of what you are, and the power of Father, Son, and Holy Spirit in you. Do you ever contemplate, take time to recognize that your home is holy because of *you*, because of your spouse, because of your children. We take little time to reverence what is most important. The most important ministry is the family. All else will pass, but the time you spend with one another is holy time, is sacred time.

We are called to be contemplatives, to be like Mary, to treasure and hallow and reflect. Think of Simeon and Anna, the senior citizens of the Gospel who spent so much time in prayer. The Holy Spirit came upon them so they were present and recognized Jesus. The Holy Spirit is upon each one of us, but so often we forget the power of the Spirit, to recognize the presence of Christ in each of the persons in our lives, in our families.

Most of us acknowledge too small a family. We only think of our blood family. But if we call God our Father, then everyone is a member of my family. This is the great gift of Jesus. He has given us not only Himself, He has given us His Father, He has given us one another. He has made us holy.

In Joseph's Silence

What is the most joyful, the happiest, moment in the New Testament? Jean Vanier, the founder of L'Arche for the adult mentally handicapped, claims that the moment of the Gospel when the angel told Joseph he could bring Mary home and have her as his wife was the most joyful. With this good news, Joseph immediately ran to his donkey, hopped on, and said "Giddyap!" Can you picture that? Joseph, the quiet man. He speaks not one word in Scripture. He's not a man of words, but he is a man of action. How many bear the name of Joseph? It's good we still have a few Joseph's around.

What must have been the joy of Joseph? What was his preparation for the birth of Jesus? How did he companion Mary? It's not as our Christmas cards show it: simple, beautiful, easy. Palestine at that time was occupied by an imperial power. They called for a census, and even though Mary was very close to giving birth, Joseph took her with him to Bethlehem, a ninety mile walk from Nazareth. What must have been his concern, his anxiety? Imagine as they walked through Jerusalem into Bethlehem four miles south of the city. Joseph was surely very preoccupied. Where could he find a place for Mary, for the birth of her child. When he finally found a place, he was quickly moved on. The angel again appeared to him reporting that some were trying to destroy the child.

So Joseph became a refugee, head of a refugee family in Egypt, and was probably unemployed. Perhaps we can better experience this if we think of him as a father in downtown Detroit with a sign "I'll work for food." Imagine Joseph's worry, anxiety, and his scrambling in order to provide food for the family. They were a homeless family, a refugee family. They were foreigners, did not know the language. Imagine someone out to murder your child. What fear, what terror, they underwent.

Also imagine, earlier in their relationship, Joseph already engaged to Mary. When the angel appeared to Mary and announced to her that she would be the mother of Emmanuel, Mary went immediately to her cousin Elizabeth. Evidently she didn't even tell Joseph because she knew he could not understand. When Mary returned from Ein Karem where Elizabeth lived, it was obvious she was with child. What went through Joseph's mind and heart in having his wife with child before they had lived together. He was a just man, and by law he had to put her aside. How many sleepless nights Joseph must have gone through! Then at last, the moment when, in a dream, the angel told him to take Mary into his home. What exuberance Joseph must have felt!

I wonder what then took place in the conversations of Mary and Joseph. How did Joseph talk to Mary? How did Mary talk to Joseph? What could they say? Perhaps much of their communication was through silences, those special kinds of silences that are too deep for any words. Who could Mary tell of her situation? Who could she turn to? Who could comfort her? What an extraordinary man Joseph must have been to be chosen by God, to be the one who would companion Mary, to be the one through whom Jesus would learn to be a man. No man has ever been as blessed as Joseph, though we have not one word from Joseph.

I think Joseph stands for all the good husbands and fathers of our time. This seems to be the age of women, the age when fathers and husbands are often silent, often reticent. What can they say? What can they claim? Perhaps we need to put more focus upon Joseph. The silent man. The worker. The homeless. The refugee. Joseph was a man of immense joy. He was a man of presence. What an immense presence he must have had with Mary. What a support and joy. Imagine how Jesus discovered who He was through His foster father, Joseph. I think that when Jesus gave the example of the good shepherd, He was thinking of His father, Joseph, and how Joseph had shepherded Him all the days of His life.

Isaiah with his prophesies is spellbinding. John the Baptist is extraordinary. We'll never appreciate Mary enough. But how good it is to know of Joseph and to remember the special Josephs in our lives. The quiet man. The resourceful person. The one whose silence is spoken deeper than any words.

Joseph had an angel, as Mary had an angel. All of us have angels. What dreams Joseph must have dreamed! What prayers he must have spoken without any words! What wonderful presence he must have been for Mary and the Child. Let us remember Joseph, and discover the hidden Joseph in each of us. Let us recognize those special Josephs who were with us in the critical moments of our lives. Imagine Jesus' joy in Joseph. Imagine the love of Mary for Joseph. This is a hidden part of our Christmas story. Silence is the hidden part of our preparation. Take and treasure those silent moments. In the stillness of the night when the reality of Jesus comes to you most deeply, remember Joseph and discover his hidden presence, his deep silence in your life and in your deepest preparation for the birth of Jesus.

NEVER TO ASK AGAIN: DO YOU LOVE ME?

How has your week been? Has it been a special week? Did you take time to believe? When do you believe? When do you exercise your faith? We spend forty days in preparation for Easter. Sometimes we forget that we prolong it for fifty more days — until Pentecost. Really, this is the more important time of the liturgical year. We call it the "mystagogia" time. All those who have been baptized and received into the Church continue for a whole year trying to immerse themselves ever more deeply into the mystery, the gift, the astonishment of their faith.

Remember Thomas and his surprise when Jesus appeared. There is a Thomas in each of us. Jesus knows that. How astonishing it is that Jesus comes for the Thomas in each of us!

I wonder where Thomas had been when Jesus first came to the apostles. Perhaps Thomas was celebrating in his own way. Perhaps he wondered whether it had all been a dream, whether it had really happened at all. Perhaps he was relieved to get out from under it; he now didn't have to do anything further. But imagine his chagrin and disappointment when the disciples said, "We have seen the Lord!"

This week, did you see the Lord? Did you see any sign of the resurrection? Was anything enkindled within you?

Perhaps out of his disappointment, Thomas exaggerated when he said, "I will never believe unless I can put my finger into His hand and my hand into His side." Would any of us dare say that? Perhaps we can be grateful to Thomas that he said it for us.

You would think then that Thomas would be the last one Jesus would bother about. But, eight days later, Jesus came and said to the disciples, "Peace be with you." Do you have that Easter peace, that peace to know that death is abolished? Life does not end with the grave. What lies ahead is far greater than we have already experienced. Sin and death have no power because Jesus is risen from the dead and He is with us.

But Thomas said he could not believe, so Jesus came — apparently just for Thomas — and said, "Take your finger. Put it into my wounds. And put your hand into my side." Then Thomas uttered that wonderful cry, "My Lord and my God!" Do you allow the Thomas within you dare to cry out, "My Lord and my God!" How would you say that? It's a wonderful phrase to try to practice. How would you whisper it? How would you shout it? Perhaps it might be good to practice it in your car. "My Lord and my God!"

As the consecrated bread and consecrated wine was elevated, in the old days, they would cry it aloud. I always whisper it to myself, "My Lord and my God."

What is this faith of ours? How do we exercise it? How do we deepen it? How do we let the cumulative faith of 2,000 years make a difference? What was your Easter grace? How did you allow it to touch you? How do you cry out, "My Lord and my God," with a new depth, with a new faith, with a new kind of peace?

I asked one of the married deacons who visits me frequently, "What was your Easter grace?" He paused for a moment and said, "You know what really struck me this year as never before is that we never have to ask Jesus again, 'Do you love me?'." We never have to ask Jesus again, "Do you love me?" If we allowed ourselves to experience the washing of our feet with water and the bathing of our whole body in His blood, if we allowed ourselves to in some way be pierced with the stigmata of Jesus, then never again do we have to ask Him, "Do you love me?"

Yesterday I drove down to Cleveland to visit a priest friend of mine who has recently had a very serious medical operation and almost died. For over fifteen years, he's been living in the oldest part of Cleveland, Central Avenue and East 35th Street. A few years ago they started building Habitat Houses. They now have built twenty Habitat Houses. Each person in the program commits to the sweat equity of 500 hours of work on someone else's house. Now the city is building 40 new private housing sites. One of the superintendents said, "We're doing this because across the street they built 20 houses for the poorest of the poor." What a wonderful sign of resurrection! There are so many signs in our everyday life, but we will not see them unless we are ready, unless we expect that Jesus will show Himself to us. He said, "I will continue to manifest myself to you."

Every Thursday night from 9:30 to 10:30, the seminarians and faculty join together for a long, loving look at the Eucharist. As I recently prepared for that holy hour, the question came to me, "How long did it take for those first priests to know what Jesus had done for them?" Jesus asked them, "Do you understand what I have done for you?" Two thousand years later, do we understand what Jesus has done and is doing for us? I wonder how long it took them to do what Jesus told them to do, "Do this in memory of me." I wonder when they washed each other's feet again, or was that too much, something that only Jesus would dare to do? I had a question for these young men preparing for the priesthood: If they knew, when they celebrated their first Eucharist, that within 24 hours they would die violently, would they do it? Jesus celebrated only one Eucharist, and He knew the price of that Eucharist was that He would die violently before the next day's sun set. I wonder if we are ready to "do" the Eucharist.

This week seven Jesuits were murdered in Africa. We don't know how many sisters and lay people. What an Easter for them! Where and how would you like to die? When Bishop Romero on the 25th of March, 1980, was celebrating Eucharist, he was machine-gunned down. I envied him. I would like to die celebrating the Eucharist. I think that in some way, whether you recognize it or not, all of us want to die celebrating the Eucharist, each day to cry out, "My Lord and my God," and to know that in some way we carry the wounds of Jesus. Perhaps, more accurately, he carries our wounds, no matter what they are of heart, of mind, of family, of work.

How good it would be for us to develop a new habit of the heart. How rarely do we take time to exercise our faith. There are a number of parishes which are beginning to understand more deeply the need for personal, intimate relationship with Jesus. They are working to do what He has asked them to do: to be His presence among those who are most in need. So many have committed themselves to an hour of adoration each week, just to exercise their faith, to allow themselves to be filled with the mystery of Jesus' presence. We never take enough time to believe. Each one of us has to be able to cry out, "We have seen the Lord." We must recognize that He comes to each of us when we doubt the most, and once again He calls us, "Put your finger into my hand, your hand into my side, and dare to believe." Join Thomas to find that depth of faith by which we cry out, "My Lord, my God."

THE ORDINARY EXTRAORDINARY FATHER

We never have enough time to celebrate the "ordinary" in our lives. Each day should be your birthday, your anniversary, a day to commemorate yourself, your family, your children, your spouse, your mother, your father. Fatherhood is one of the important roles we most often fail to acclaim. Fathers should be recognized more than once each year. Every day we should proclaim, "Happy Father's Day!"

Happy Father's Day. I wonder how many fathers are happy. How do we get into Father's Day? Do we take a long loving look at the reality of fatherhood? We don't have very much time to think and we are not very inclined to it, especially when it comes to something so close to us. Despite how difficult it is to step back and look at the common, the ordinary, the simple, it is very good to do so. There is something marvelous about celebrating what is in us. So often Our Lord said, "If you but knew the gift of God. . . ." We never have enough time to celebrate. We take so little time to contemplate, to take a long loving look at reality. Ten minutes on Father's Day is never enough, but what an important day it is. Paul in his letter to the Ephesians says, "I kneel before the Father from whom every fatherhood in heaven and earth takes its name" (3:14-15). Isn't it wonderful that a man shares with God God's own identity? What is it to be father? What are you celebrating on Father's Day?

What do you remember of your father? What will your children remember about you as father?

Ours is an age of discovery of the father. As women become more and more fathers, fathers are becoming more and more mothers. But the one thing a woman can never do, is *be* father, anymore than a man can be mother.

How have you been fathered? How are you fathering? My father was 35 when he had his first son: me. He died when I was 34. I never caught up to him. I never had enough time with my father. I spend a lot of time with him now. What a delight it is to discover the heart of one's father. We all leave home. Sometimes long before we are ready. We go to many different and strange lands. We discover who we are. We begin to recognize what has been given to us, and sometimes there is a turning around, a moment when we turn and realize what we had.

And what it is to turn around and to return home, to return to the heart of our father — not our human father, but the Father who is always with us. Jesus spoke about nothing more than He spoke of His Father. He shared, "I am never alone. The Father is always with me. I can do nothing of myself. It is the Father living in me."

How long does it take to discover our human father? How long does it take to discover our heavenly Father, our Father not only in heaven but who has come and made His home in each of us?

What I remember most about my father, what I am most grateful to him for is that he led me to the Father. The most constant memory I have of my father is that he knelt in prayer. He never taught me to pray. He never told me to pray. He simply prayed. I think my father reached that point where he knew he was inadequate as a father. There was so much more than he could bring to me, than he could give by himself.

I remember when I was appointed spiritual father at the Seminary. I never dreamt that would happen. Yet, what a joy when I was told I would be spiritual father to so many men. I have hundreds of spiritual sons. When I began, I was consumed with great excitement imagining all I'd be able to say to them and to teach them and do. That was the first stage. What joy and excitement in our time when fatherhood is deliberate, not simply by providence. What a point in a man's life when he deliberately chooses to take on the role of father, when he believes he has something to pass on, when he feels that the world is worth his genes and the sons and daughters he will bring forth. What a beautiful moment it is when a man is no longer living for himself, when he wants to pass on, out of gratitude and out of wonder, what he has been given. He becomes generative. He knows he can pass on his life. That is a wonderful beginning.

However, there comes a point, which I experienced in my own "fatherhood" as spiritual father, when we realize it isn't enough to have shining ideas and inspirations. We realize that it isn't sufficient to touch the heart of a person. We discover that it is not what I could do, but what I had to become that really matters.

It seems that motherhood, on one level, is much easier than fatherhood. Motherhood is so "hands on." The mother carries the child within herself. She cannot escape from her motherhood. It is much more difficult for a man because a man can run away. There is an escape to fatherhood because fathering is not so much "doing" or even "breadwinning," as it is "being." A father soon realizes that what is important is not what he does but who he is and who he is becoming and what desires he is creating in his sons and daughters to become who he is.

There is a distance in fatherhood unlike the intense closeness of motherhood. There is not the same kind of intimacy. There are so many things a father has to do. He is drawn in so many different ways. It seems that a mother's instinct is deeper, more tangible. A father is not wired for fathering. The mystery of being a father. The mystery of claiming the same name as God has. How awesome it is to be a father! What a struggle. How long does it take to become a father? Most men feel insecure, inadequate. They are very competent at their jobs, but what is harder than to really enter into closeness, to be connected? What do you do with little kids? What do you do with grown kids? How deep is the need to have some idea of who I can become, of what will become of me!

A father worries because he feels he knows so much of what's happening in our world, in the world to which his children must be exposed. Fathers are plunged into an awareness of what's coming down the road, somehow attuned to impending trials in fathering and caring for his children. A father has to be the "hammer" that works the "metal." When one works with metal, it must be pounded to make it become hard. If it is pounded too hard then it can break, but if it's too soft it cannot do its work. A father recognizes the need to hammer himself while maintaining a tenderness and sensitivity. How does a man hammer himself into something hard enough and yet soft enough?

Fathers show concern in a different way than mothers do. How much they have to make of themselves in order to create in their children a desire and an awareness of what they can become. Jesus prayed to His Father, "Deliver us from evil." How much evil a father wants to protect his children from! "Lead us not into temptation." He knows where he has been. He knows of terrible things that can happen. How does he help his children to be strong enough to overcome that evil and that temptation? "Forgive us our sins." How a father prays over his children that he be forgiven his own sins, his own wounds passed on by his own father. We never know how much our fathers have overcome in themselves and have not passed on. How much will their children not struggle with because the father has hammered himself, has died to so much in himself to free his children. What a gift! How much we never had to struggle with because our fathers overcame it in themselves.

How does one develop within oneself the resources? How does one grow as a father? How does a father really get to his children? I think every father breathes into his son or his daughter the desire to be more than he was, to be a better father, to be a better mother, to be a better parent. To be a father means one accepts limitations. Only when one becomes a father does one realize how much his father let go of in order that he could be a father — to give away so much of his freedom, to give away so much of what he could have done. There is a stage of exuberance of being a father, a stage of coming to know that I have to die. The father chooses to accept so many limitations, to let go so much freedom because he chooses to become a father; biologically and spiritually.

How to discover one's own father? Every one of us in one way or another leaves home. Sometimes we can't wait to get out from under. We go to many countries, many strange places. What a wonderful moment it is when we, like the prodigal son who runs out of everything, begin to remember and want to go back to our father's house. The prodigal son knows he's no longer a son but he wants to go back. And the only reason he did that is because of the prayer of his father reaching out to him and drawing him back, letting him know there was a place for him. What a moment that is when a father begins to realize that something is missing. Why was his son compelled to leave home? Why was he drawn to so many different and strange places? But through it all, his father continued to love him. Imagine the immense welcome. What is it when we return to our home? What is it when we discover the Father who has always been with us, who has always believed and hoped and loved us? What is it to discover the heart of our heavenly Father? To return home and discover anew what it is to be son.

So "Happy Father's Day!" every day. Who are these holy men in our midst who are fathers and are aware of the sacrament of becoming a father, who know they cannot do it of themselves. They are drawn to kneel before their Father who is in heaven and in their own hearts. Who are these men who, through their own children, are born again and again? Who are these called by their children to be what they would never choose to be of themselves? Holy men.

We have "holy fathers." They are in touch with their heavenly Father. There is no way of being truly father unless you are truly priest, unless you are a spiritual father, unless you breathe a spirit into your sons and daughters so that they can become all that they can become. They are so dependent upon what you are and what you are becoming. How important it is for fathers to reach that stage of sacrament, of priesthood, and to recognize that every day a father says, "This is my body. This is my time. This is my life. This is my energy... given for you." The father who no longer has to live for himself and does his Eucharist in his work, in his neighborhood, and says, "This is my blood shed for you." "If you but knew the gift of God and who it is that lives in you."

One of the special joys I had in the Holy Land was to hear Hebrew and Arabic being spoken and to understand it when the little children ran around saying, "Abba. Abba. Abba." "Daddy. Daddy. Daddy." The greatest joy of the Father is when his children cry out to Him, "Abba. Abba. Abba."

To Shine Like the Sun

I love a magnificent sunrise. There is something so overwhelming with the sunrise. One never gets used to sunrises or sunsets because every sunrise and every sunset is unique. There's never been one like another since the beginning of time.

Ours is the first generation who has been able to see the "earthrise" from the surface of the moon — either on television or in photos. What an incredible moment to see this blue jewel rise from the surface of the moon. Some of us may, some day, have that experience first hand. How moving it is to be aware that we are *on* that blue jewel that is rotating a thousand miles every hour in an orbit around the sun. How insignificant each one of us seems in terms of sunrise and earthrise, and yet, we are more important than sunrise or earthrise, and one day we will shine even greater than the sun in the kingdom of heaven.

Every time we gather together, we are waiting. We wait not just for an hour in prayer, but we wait for the final rising. What will it be when we experience the mystery that has been hidden in our lives — the great secret that we have always carried within us, that God has sown in us. We carry this immense secret, this sacrament, this mystery. If we could but recognize who we are, the treasure in us: the kingdom of heaven!

Jesus came to help us understand and to experience and to live more consciously that great mystery, that wonderful secret that He is in us. We are pilgrims of an immense journey. Every day, every hour, every week, we become closer. The kingdom of heaven is like the smallest seed, the mustard seed, that is planted in us and is intended to grow and to become immense. The kingdom of heaven is like the yeast that makes the bread rise, but so often in our lives we can seem so insignificant. What difference does our life, or any life, make? For this reason, we must allow the seed, the Word of God, to have its effect in us and to nurture us. We must allow that seed to grow in its fullness.

Jesus speaks about the kingdom of heaven. We pray often "Thy kingdom come." Is it coming? Where is the kingdom? Can you see it? How is it coming? Jesus tells us that we are the kingdom of heaven. "The kingdom of heaven is in you." How are we changing? How are we growing? Is the kingdom of heaven in me? If so, where? What is that kingdom?

The kingdom is Jesus' presence. We are drawn because we are people of faith. In our gathering, we become aware that we are waiting, we are waiting for the end of the world, we are waiting for the fullness of the kingdom.

We are the most visible manifestation of the kingdom when we gather in faith, but that is not enough. The kingdom is to continue to grow. It is not enough to receive the Body and Blood of Christ only for a moment. The kingdom is to be in our hearts, in our minds, in our hands, in our feet. If we could only dare to believe this truth, this secret, this mystery hidden from the beginning of creation. That secret, that sacrament, that mystery is Christ in you. You are called to be more and more that kingdom. You are to shine greater than the sun, more brilliant than any sunrise or sunset or earthrise or earthset. Just imagine that little blue jewel orbiting the sun. How insignificant, how utterly invisible we are from the moon, or from a few miles overhead. Yet, the kingdom of heaven is in us. Jesus is in us. What an incredible journey we are on. The journey into the kingdom. The journey into Eucharist. Where are you in that journey? How does that little mustard seed, that small particle of bread and a few drops of wine, His presence, Body and Blood — how does He grow in you? How did He grow in you last week? How does He want to grow in you this week? The awesome responsibility of living on a new level of consciousness! The world has not seen nor heard nor touched Christ's presence in us.

Much of my time is spent working around the country in small groups with people who want to grow spiritually, who in some way are stirred by the mystery of what it is to be Christian. They in some way want to, not only have a notion, but experience the kingdom of heaven within themselves. We can be so often discouraged by ourselves. We can be caught in that Jonah complex of running away from our own goodness, our own holiness. So often we are more conscious of the weeds than the wheat. We are so often unaware of what is growing in us, what is happening to us. We try so hard to do good. We try to be faithful, but the weeds keep coming and we see in our own lives that the good we want to do, we do not find ourselves doing, and the evil we want to avoid, we find ourselves doing. There is no way of eliminating human weakness. Paul writes out of his own experience that when we cannot pray, when we feel so downcast and depressed about our weakness, when we feel least worthy, the Spirit comes to us and enables us to pray, to begin again, to continue on the journey. There are so many good people who get very discouraged and consider themselves as insignificant, as nothing. There is always that temptation of running away from our goodness, our holiness, and to think it all depends upon ourselves. What Jesus said again and again is that it does not just depend upon ourselves. He is always coming to us. He is always doing something new in us. No matter what our sin or weaknesses may be, we are to never be discouraged, never to lose confidence, because He is with us. He is doing something wonderful in us. Even though we do not see or feel because His grace is so deep, so hidden, He continues to invite us and He promises us that He will always be with us. We are never surprised — or perhaps sometimes we are — at the weaknesses and sins within ourselves, but far more should be our surprise that we continue to come to Jesus, that we come to Him again and again, that we have a hunger and a thirst for the Eucharist, that our ears are opened to hear the Word once again. We never know when we take that step that makes us a saint, a holy person. You are a holy person. You cannot deny it. You are holy because the kingdom of God is already in you. Again and again He comes to you. Your light is already shining brighter than the sun because of the secret, the mystery, the sacrament that you are. As you receive His Body and Blood recognize who you are and live what you see.

Every day and every moment in the day, God is looking upon us, loving us, carrying our heart within His own heart. Jesus' experience of God the Father was that He was never alone, but that the Father was always with Him. Each one of us is invited to Jesus' experience of the Father. That makes us Christians: to accept His invitation to follow Him, to realize that He is always with us, He is always loving us, He is always calling us to a deeper, richer consciousness. He is doing something wonderful within us, and we are called to dare to believe that. No matter what our weaknesses may be, no matter what our faults or sins may be, He sends His Holy Spirit into us. In the midst of our weaknesses, when we cannot pray, His Spirit grows within us with unutterable sounds. It is so good to experience our own waiting, waiting for our lives to be lived out. We are this week, one week closer than last week. We are time limited. We are called to grow each day, each week. We are called to be the kingdom. When we gather, we gather to look into the mirror of who we are. Jesus is planting the kingdom in the world, and we are the plant, the seed, His presence. He wants the whole world to come to new life. He wants the day star to rise in our hearts and for our faces to reflect the glory of His Father. The kingdom of heaven is in us. The seed is the bearer of immense fruit. We are not alone. He is tending us, caring for us, and He would that we shine more wonderfully than the sun, reflecting the secret, the mystery, the sacrament that we are. We are on the way. His life is in us and He will see to it that we bear fruit abundantly. Let us allow the Spirit to draw us into a prayer that we could never pray alone, and recognize that the kingdom is alive and our life is in Christ Jesus.

It is not easy to become conscious. It is so easy to be half awake, to be semiconscious. But what a wonderful thing it is to begin to feel a fascination, a curiosity, to make sense out of life and to live our life "fired" rather than cold and empty.

I was recently in Indiana where 28 people had come together to commit themselves to a three year program of spiritual growth. They would spend 12 weekends at their own cost to nurture, share, and grow in their faith. I listened to them tell their stories. Some were couples: one 40 years married, another just married. Some of them were very affluent, some of them very poor. But something brought them together, and they were committing themselves for three year, for twelve weekends. One man commented, "I've never felt so foolish in all my life. This is so unpredictable of me. No one would believe it of me. I don't dare tell anyone." But I was so impressed with him.

There is something happening to all of us. Again and again, the Lord comes to us. He comes at every stage of our life. Some of us begin to respond to His call at dawn, some at midday, some in the late afternoon of our lives. We are called to go into the vineyard. We are all called to discover that life is Christ, or it is nothing.

You are holy. You are a holy person. That is because you seek God. Sometimes we do not know what we are seeking, but we are called to an increase in faith. We are called to live our lives as evidence of the Gospel. Yes, it is easier to take the road that everyone else is on. It is easier to let our faith linger at a minimum survival level. It is easier to be a cradle Catholic. It is easy to never get out of the crib, to never learn how to talk, to never learn how to share our faith. It is easy to never receive the faith, life, and fire of others.

Once again today, Jesus comes. Wherever we are in our life,

whatever level of consciousness or unconsciousness, He asks us, "Why do you stand around idle so much of your life? Go into the vineyard." We are all in that late hour, that last hour. How much has been done by generations before us! How many martyrs! How many have lived such extraordinary faith! And we of the last hour: how little we have to do as workers in the vineyard!

MORE MAGNIFICENT THAN ST. PETER'S BASILICA

In each of us there is something that waits. We are always looking for something more. We are always hungry for something more. Nothing that we do or see or hear or taste or feel can fill the immense longing and waiting that is within us. "Make ready the way of the Lord!" What valley do we have to fill, what mountain bring down, what obstacles to remove in order to see and hear and feel what God is doing?

One Sunday morning — the First Sunday of Advent, 1995 — I was sitting in St. Peter's Basilica in Rome to celebrate the installation of cardinals. We had to be there an hour and half before the Mass began to get through security and find our places. Although we sat there waiting and waiting and waiting, it was not difficult. St. Peter's Basilica is so fascinating, so dramatic, so immense, that one could spend the whole day and not get tired. There could be twenty parish churches put in St. Peter's aisle and it would not be filled. I recalled an old Italian peasant who, walking into St. Peter's for the first time, looked intently around and remarked, "Not bad for a fisherman!" But as one's eye is captivated by the beauty and the magnificence of that great basilica, one could not but recognize that nothing is too good for the Lord. What a beautiful symbol of the men and women who wanted to do something beautiful for God in His magnificence! How much we can admire those people of three or four centuries ago, for whom nothing was too good to honor Our Lord. The extravagance of their art and their building is rather awesome, and each one feels insignificant in terms of the Basilica's grandeur and splendor.

How exciting when the trumpets blew and the procession began! We watched as cardinal after cardinal — thirty from all over the whole world — passed closely in front of us. I could almost reach out and touch Pope John Paul II as he slowly walked that immense aisle of St. Peter's Basilica. The music brought an anticipation of the heavenly choir. St. Peter's seems intended to give us a taste of heaven and what is to come.

As I waited there, many thoughts came to me. One thought was that Jesus never went to Rome. Jesus traveled very little His whole life. Perhaps no further than between Detroit and Port Huron. How limited Jesus was. He never went to those far away places with strange sounding names. However, as I thought further, Jesus did go to Rome, in Peter and in Paul. During my visit, we saw the places where Peter was crucified upside down and Paul beheaded. We walked through the catacombs where so many of the saints suffered for their faith, where we could still see the mark of the grave diggers of over two thousand years ago.

I lived four years in Rome, and many times I was in that Basilica. I could look over to the left to see the tomb of Pope Pius X. I attended his canonization. I thought of all the canonizations of saints, all the centuries of celebrations held there in St. Peters. I anticipated the day when our own Fr. Solanus will be declared a saint, and I hope to be there.

The magnificence of the liturgy that day in St. Peter's Basilica is impossible to describe! Yet, as I reflected, I'm sure that Pope John Paul does not know my name. Of those thirty cardinals from all over the world, two of them know me by name: our own Cardinal Maida and a classmate of mine with whom I spent three years in Rome, Cardinal Wheeler of Baltimore. So there were two of perhaps 20,000 people who knew my name. The most important moment of the whole liturgy, of that whole morning, was the moment when Jesus became flesh once again upon that altar. The most important moment of the day came when the Basilica became quiet and once again a priest-Pope said the words, "This is my Body given for you. This is my Blood to be shed for you."

The Holy Father did not come to shake my hand, but Jesus came to me, and He knows my name. He knows me as no one else has ever known me and He loves me. The most important thing that happened that Sunday morning, among the magnificence of the celebration, was that Jesus came to me. Nothing was more important.

Each Sunday morning, each liturgy, you experience the same important thing that happened to me at St. Peter's that Sunday: Jesus comes to you. I may not know your name, but Jesus does. He knows the whole of your life. Jesus did not need a basilica. A cave, a stable was enough. You may not see yourself as the Basilica of St. Peter, you may experience yourself as merely a cave or manger. Jesus seems to be much more comfortable in almost nothing. He is coming to each of us in a new way. Each one of us has something of John the Baptist. Each one of us can do so much to allow Him to come and live in us and through us, to be His presence. How many are looking to us? that we might be some kind of light in their darkness? some kind of joy in their despair? some kind of light in their nothingness?

Sometimes I've wondered: if I were God, how would I come upon earth? The last thing I would ever imagine is to come as an infant, to come powerless, to come as "nobody." Yet this is the way Jesus comes to us. He comes totally powerless. He comes as an infant. For two thousand years, Jesus hasn't said anything, hasn't done anything, He is just present. He is Emmanuel, God with us. We don't need to go to Rome. We don't need to go to Lourdes, to Fatima, to Guadalupe, because we could never really go to Him. We could never find Him. He is the one who comes to us. He is the one who finds us no matter how mixed up our lives are, no matter how many valleys, holes, we have created, no matter how many obstacles we have set up. Jesus is coming. There is within each of us immense longing, an immense need to see and to taste and to touch Jesus.

The heart of our being is a longing and waiting for God. Nothing else will ever satisfy, because He has made us for Himself. He has made us for ourselves. He has made us for one another. The wonder and magnificence of St. Peter's Basilica is that it is a mirror, a reflection of who and what each one of us is. If we could only believe the significance and the importance of each one of us! The Lord has no favorites. Many have special positions, but only Jesus knows us by name. He is the only one who comes to be with us always. It's so hard for us to believe. We have the notion and idea in our head, but to really believe that the God of the Universe has become human! None of us adequately believe. At this moment the earth is turning on its axis at the rate of 1000 miles per hour. Before this liturgy is over, we will have traveled 1000 miles in rotation. And the earth is about to finish another revolution of the sun. The diameter of that orbit is 186 million miles. No wonder we're tired. We know and recognize so little of what is happening at every moment of our lives. But this is new time, new space, and we're called to listen to the word of God, to disentangle ourselves, to remodel, to fill those holes we create in our lives, to overcome the obstacles that in some way prevent us from recognizing who we are, whom we are called to become. Jesus comes. Once again, there is a new cycle to our lives. Jesus rarely comes dramatically. He doesn't overwhelm us. He comes so simply that you really have to strain your eyes and your ears and your heart to recognize who it is. How gently He comes to us!

On December 8, during Advent each year, we celebrate the Feast of the Immaculate Conception. Have you ever thought of yourself at the first moment of your own conception? Do you ever think of how big you were at that first moment? You were submicroscopic. Imagine your father and your mother waiting for those nine long months for you to be born. Something of us in the womb could not wait to be born. The rest of our story is how we wait all throughout our lives. We can't wait until we get to school. We can't wait until we get out of school. We can't wait to get married, to have children. Then we can't wait to get the children out of the house. We're always waiting. How do you wait for God? A beautiful reading of Paul (1 Cor 13) calls upon us to enter into a new knowledge, a new understanding, a new wisdom. It is so important to get in touch with what is deepest within ourselves so we can do what Paul asks: to value the better things. We are so busy. It's so good to try to get in touch with what we are longing for.

Jesus comes to you. Not Pope John Paul, not Cardinal Maida, not even your pastor, nor myself can come to you in the way that Jesus does. He is coming as never before because this is a new Advent, a new Christmas. What do you want for Christmas? What do you want to give to Him? What does He want to give to you?

Be ready. Prepare, because He is coming to you. "Maranatha." Come, Lord Jesus. Come. Let us try to taste and to experience that deepest part of ourselves that is longing and yearning for Him who knows us by name and comes to give us the gift of Himself, the gift of ourselves, the gift of one another. If we could only believe the truth.

The Epiphany Banquet

Do You Have a Star?

Advent begins the New Year of the Church. It is a time to be alert, to be on guard, to be awake. It is a period of waiting, a time of grace, a time of Advent grace. What are *you* waiting for? We have a liturgical calendar that again and again breaks into the "sleeping sickness" of the soul and invites us to become alive in a new way and to think more deeply and to stir up our hopes that there is something more to us, something more to life than the ordinary every day.

Advent brings with it a new perspective and the grace to recognize with new eyes. There are signs we should be watching for. We must be alert, awake, and eager for a new dawning of Christ in our lives. He is always coming more deeply and more radically into our lives, but we can get so used to Jesus that we overlook Him. It can be dangerous to see the truth and to act upon it. Most of us are more comfortable with the automatic pilot. We just go from day to day, week to week, month to month, year to year — and it doesn't seem to make a difference. It is so hard to open our eyes. It is even more difficult to open our souls and our hearts.

On the first day of Advent, can we truly say, "Happy New Year"? What is so happy about it? Will it be the same thing all over again? Are we going to continue in sameness? Are we ready for something new? What is new in your life? Have you found any new light? new joy? new hope? Are you more alive than you were this time last year? Is there anything new? anything exciting? anything you feel called to give yourself to?

Advent brings waiting. We are waiting for a new light. We are waiting for a new phenomenon. Especially in our season of Advent, we should be like little children and allow ourselves to be excited, to be searching for a new manifestation, a new hearing of the Word of God, a new change in our lives. Do you sense yourself waiting? looking? What are you looking for? What is your quest? What is your dream? Do you expect anything new from God? anything new from or for yourself? Do you respond to the "little child" within you leaping for joy when something new is detected?

We know what faith is. We exercise it through our prayer, liturgy, Eucharist. We know what love is. We experience it through our varied relationships. We know that we are to love one another as Jesus has loved us. But perhaps the most forgotten virtue, the one least exercised, least valued, is hope. Yet how important it is to hope and to dream! to dream dreams and be willing to pay the price to allow them to become true! What is your hope? What is your dream? Or do you think of your life and dreams as mostly behind you? What expectations do you have?

What do you look for? What are you longing for? Do you ever take the time to get in touch with what is deepest within you? Our days are so full. We seem to always be on the run, perhaps more during Advent than any other time of the year. There is never enough time. It is good that at least we have an hour on the weekend to come to church, to sit, to listen, perhaps to dream, and perhaps to hope. How do you hope? How do you search the depths of your inmost being? What does Jesus awaken within you?

What has happened in your life this year? How much light and joy and hope did you touch, or how much debris did you allow to accumulate within yourself? What a wonderful thing it is to have an awe of God — and a wonder about God. Do you once in a while ask yourself, "What if it's true? What if there really is a God? and that He knows me by name? and He is always coming into my life?" There is never a day when Jesus doesn't in some way manifest Himself to us — whether we are ready or not, seeking or not, hoping or not. This very day, in some way, He will manifest Himself to me. Will I be open? Will I really see? Will I finally recognize that I am surrounded by God?

Recall the Scripture passage of the young man who asked, "Lord, what must I do to be saved?" Scripture tells us that Jesus looked at the young man "with love." Have you allowed yourself to experience Jesus looking at you with love? Are you loved? Are you desired? Are you known by God? By Father, Son, and Holy Spirit? Did you ever expect to meet Him in this life? Are you aware that you are not only surrounded by God, but that He is in you? "I will come to you and my Father will come to you, and we will make our home in you." There is nothing more exciting than having a sense of God, a hunger for God, a thirst for God. It is so easy to let the everyday take over our lives, to allow each day to be just like another day. But the tradition of the Church always tries to interrupt our lives, to break into our lives, and to invite us to new possibilities. So at the dawn of each Advent we say, "Happy New Year! Happy new year of grace! Happy hoping and searching and waiting!"

During Advent we listen to the words of Isaiah, the prophet of the sixth century before Jesus. His writings are considered almost a fifth Gospel. We hear about John the Baptist, that he was called to recognize Jesus and to proclaim Him. We hear the stories of Mary and Joseph. At Christmas we hear about the shepherds. At Epiphany, about the kings and the magi. With which of these do you identify?

Imagine those shepherds in the Judaean hills a month before the census that would bring Jesus and Mary and Joseph to Bethlehem. It was probably just another ordinary year. They probably didn't anticipate anything special. Imagine their surprise when angels appeared to them and told them that a savior was born for them. Is there something of the shepherd in you in your ordinary life? Is there something that you still look for and long for?

Or do you think of yourself as a magi, one of those astronomers of ancient time, who followed the star that led them to Bethlehem? Those magi who would follow the star, who knew the signs of the heaven, may have been journeying for several years before Jesus was born. Do you have a star? What guides you? What are you led by? What do you look for? Jesus is already here, but He is always awakening us to His presence more deeply and more clearly.

Do you think of Mary and Joseph leaving Nazareth and winding their way down the Jordan Valley to Bethlehem to fulfill the Roman emperor's call for a census? Do you imagine what this time was like for Mary? that last month she carried Jesus within her womb? Each of us through the Eucharist and the Word of God carry Him within ourselves. In some way we are meant to bring Him to others. We prepare ourselves through prayer. When we light our Advent wreath at the altar, in our homes, at our dining table, when we open and listen to Scripture, we make holy this time. All the way to Christmas is Christmas.

Do we allow Jesus to live so fully in us that we cannot hold Him to ourselves but are compelled to share His good news. How many families in our communities no longer come to church! Perhaps some will come back at Christmas. Do you hold out an invitation: "Come home for Christmas. Join us in our prayer and our celebration of Christ the Lord"?

Do we prepare ourselves by helping others? What is the preparation in our family? What is our preparation relative to those we do not know, those we have forgotten, those we have been separated from? The light of Christ goes out to the whole world. Christmas will be celebrated in Moslem countries, in Israel, in Japan, in India.... Many do not know what they celebrate, but they know that it is profitable. It is very profitable to "celebrate" this Christmas feast. But, we are called to be different. It is easy to approach the infant in the crib. It is easy to celebrate the birth of a child. No one has problems with Christmas. The difficulty and the discomfort come when the child grows up. To relate to Jesus as an adult, as someone who speaks to us, as someone who has expectations of us, as someone who wants something from us: herein lies the difficulty. Jesus says, "Come follow me." Not the commercial world, or the media, but, "Come follow me." How gentle a voice! How easily lost! How easily set aside and forgotten!

And so we always need a new beginning. Advent is a perfect time to make a new beginning, to insert something new in your life, to give yourself to something as important as you are, to give yourself to seeking, tracking God. This season invites us to be more aware of the spaces within ourselves that we have never visited. How much we do not know within ourselves!

Advent's new beginning is a waiting for a fuller and deeper coming of Jesus into us, a new flash point of recognition, of conversion. Who is Jesus? Who is He in my life? How is He decisive? Is my home different because of my faith? Do I really live what I witness on Sunday morning? Has my home become a presence of Jesus? Am I different because of who He is? What has been different this year? As the year began, what did I expect or hope to happen? What was my dream or my promise? What will I do and become during this next year of grace? Will I wake up? Will I simplify my life? Will I allow time? Will I recognize what and who I already carry within myself?

The children in your lives have probably already announced what they want for Christmas. What do you want? What would bring you deep inner happiness? What does Jesus want for Christmas? How will you prepare a gift for Him? Can you imagine the gift He is preparing for you? How good it is to get in touch with our yearnings! In our inmost depths, there is an immense yearning for something more, something which can never be fulfilled in this life. We are waiting for something out of the ordinary. It is a holy moment to be in touch with the holy within ourselves, to begin again, to open ourselves to something beyond eye or ear or touch. The Lord is coming. He is already in us, but how little time we give to Him. So He comes again and again. Will Christmas make a difference? more than last Christmas? Will something begin to beat in us that has never beat before? Will we hear a new kind of music? Will we open our ears in a way we've never opened them before?

Advent is holy time. It is an especially holy time in our families. How do we counteract the secular abuse of Christmas? When we light our Advent wreaths, when we open the Word of God, when we hear the words of Isaiah, of John the Baptist, of Mary and Joseph, will we allow Him to enkindle something in us? Will we allow ourselves to wonder each day, "What can I give to Him?" and "What is He going to give to me?" Watch. Pay attention. Stir up the hope that is within you. The Lord is coming to you.

DON'T LET THEM WEAR ME OUT!

How is it going? How did it go for you this week? What has been your "it" this week? The "it" is Advent. Did you light any candles this week? Do you find a change of mood within yourself? This is "holy" time, "sacred" time, "happy" time. Are you getting in gear? Was the family Advent wreath on your table? Does your family have a crib or creche where you and the children put in straws for the good you've done during the week. I remember my sister and her children used to put one or two straws in each day, but before the day was finished, they were taking straws out. How is it going for you?

We have a holy place nearby called Mt. Tabor Monastery. There are four Dominican contemplative Sisters there. A dozen of us from the parish gathered there yesterday for a day of being, a day of prayer. Have you ever thought of what it would be to be a contemplative for a day? The Trappists, like Thomas Merton, spend their whole lives in prayer and contemplation. Imagine taking the time to be a contemplative for one day, to spend a day just in the presence of Jesus, to have nothing else to do. Mt. Tabor is a wonderful place. The Sisters are always there, always open. Imagine making a short pilgrimage to a Mt. Tabor in your area, as a family. Just deposit yourself there for a short while and allow Jesus to give you His refreshment. He is always inviting us to come, to "come all you who are labored and stressed out, and I will refresh you."

Do you ever give Jesus enough time to refresh you? How much

we need to get into a different gear! How wonderful is the tradition of the Church in Advent and Easter and Lent to call us to live on a different level of consciousness and awareness.

One of the women yesterday prayed, "Don't let them wear me out." There are so many things that can wear us out. There are so many things that can hold us at a lesser level than who we really are. It is refreshing to take time, to gather your family together, to pray a decade of the rosary. By letting go of our rich religious traditions in the home, we have become so poor. Few families recognize their poverty. I remember the father of a family who was haunted by the prayer of the Eucharist when Jesus says, "Do this in memory of me." What troubled him was his own question, "What am I doing? What am I asking my children, my family to do in remembrance of me?"

How would you like to be remembered? What are you doing that your children will do in memory of you? Advent is a special time of the year to come into a richer consciousness, an awareness that we are a holy people. Do you know how good you are and how special you are? You are people of faith. You demonstrate that often. It would be easy to stay in bed when it's cold outside, to turn over for a few more hours. But you come to Mass as a holy people, a good people, a people drawn by the Lord to come to the well, the burning bush, and to allow yourself to be enkindled, to light another candle within yourself.

During Advent, we celebrate the Feast of the Immaculate Conception, a holy day of opportunity. Do you make it a point to be here? We who are Catholic are called into a very special, intimate relationship with Mary. Each of us has an opportunity to receive the gift that Jesus gave to us from the cross when He said, "Daughter and son, behold your mother." How do we let Mary be a significant part of our prayer and our lives. The eighth of December is also the national feast of our country. It is a strange feast — for who can we tell that we are going to celebrate the Immaculate Conception? They'd respond, "You're going to celebrate the what?"

What is the Immaculate Conception? Maximilian Kolbe, the Polish priest who laid down his life for another prisoner on the 14th of August, 1944, is the contemporary theologian of the Immaculate Conception. In his writings he reflects that Mary was filled with the Holy Spirit from the first moment of her existence, from the moment of her conception.

What you know of Mary is a mirror of something about yourself. Like Mary, we are called to be filled with the Holy Spirit. Not much is said about the Holy Spirit in the Advent season, but the Holy Spirit is the heart of it all. How often we pray the Hail Mary without recognizing that it's a prayer about ourselves. When we say, "Blessed is the fruit of your womb," we are talking not only about Jesus but we are talking about ourselves. How blessed we are because Jesus has given us Mary as our mother! She carries us in her womb, the womb of her heart.

There is never a day when we are not prayed over. There is never a day of our lives that we are not "overshadowed" by the Holy Spirit — that we might give birth to something new in ourselves. As we look forward to the anniversary of Jesus' birth, we must recognize that it is not Jesus who is to be born — He has been born totally and completely. What we look forward to is a new birth of our self. We are not fully born. Perhaps the best of our self is yet to be born. We carry within ourselves an image and likeness of Jesus. That is what we are going to become. We are growing each day to be like Christ Jesus, to put Him "on" in mind and heart and body. Mary is our companion helping us to hold onto the mystery, to deepen our hope, to fulfill the dream of what we are yet to become.

The Feast of the Immaculate Conception is a holy day of opportunity — an opportunity to become fully who we are, sons and daughters who call Mary our mother. We pray, "Pray for us your children, now and at the hour of our birth." We are always coming to further birth.

The call of Advent then is to awake from the habits of our "automatic pilot." So often we go from day to day without a thought, without a reflection. We are very special people who are called to be the consciousness and the prayer in the world. Just as those four Sisters of Mt. Tabor spend their day in prayer, so each of us has something of the contemplative in us. We may not be fully conscious of it, but there is something in us, a presence of Christ in us that wants to grow, to fill our minds and our hearts and our hands and our feet. We are called to be holy. We are called to be happy. We are called to be Jesus' presence in the world. Each of us is on the way to Bethlehem, to a new birth. We are in count-down mode.

Each one of us has a need to go to Bethlehem. We already have Bethlehem within us. We have Jerusalem. We are blessed. We are the womb of Mary, the womb of her heart. We are called to become more alive, to become more conscious, to recognize the contemplative within us. It's good to ask ourselves "How is it going?", "How did it go for me this week?", "What do I want for Christmas?" "What do I want Jesus to do in me for Christmas?" "What is my hope?" "What is my dream?" "How am I drawing my whole family into my prayer, into my waiting?" Jesus is coming to us.

"Too much of a good thing, is wonderful." We will never have enough of what Jesus wants to give to us. We are not fully born. We are still in labor. So we pray again and again, "Rejoice, Mary. The Lord loves you very dearly." In that love we know that we are loved very dearly, that we are full of grace, full of the Holy Spirit. We know that as we pray, "Blessed is the fruit of your womb," we are praying over ourselves.

Whom do you bless? With your eyes, with your smile, with your heart? How are you blessing one another? How do you bless your children? We join with the whole Church in crying out, "Pray for us, your children, now and at the hour of our birth."

TELL ME AGAIN

During Advent each year, we celebrate the Feast of Our Lady of Guadalupe, the celebration of Our Lady's apparition in Mexico City. In 1531, she appeared to Juan Diego. When the bishop requested a sign, Juan brought his mantle. As he opened it before the bishop, out fell a magnificent bouquet of roses revealing the imprint of Our Lady displayed on his mantle. That event is celebrated today with our Hispanic people in our city, our diocese, and throughout the world. It's a beautiful feast of Our Lady's apparition on this continent such a short time after Columbus had discovered America.

How often we have watched our procession of candles and heard the choir draw us into a special level of joy! The Gospel says, "Rejoice in the Lord always. Pray always. Be always thankful. Be Eucharist."

What's the level of your joy today? Has it grown from Sunday to Sunday to Sunday? Do you experience some joy welling up in you? Is there any difference? Has Advent enabled you in some way to touch into that special gift of Jesus' joy? Do you show it? The most important decorating you will do this season is not your house or your tree, it is your face. You have to practice at it.

There is so much sadness in the world. Every day we're plunged into it again and again and again. It seems natural to be serious, heavy, expressionless or simply sad. We have to protest against that sadness with Jesus' prayer: "That my joy may be in you and that in you it may reach its fullness." Imagine the joy of Jesus that He carried within Himself. Imagine the wonder of it all that He should pray that "my joy may be in you and that in you it reach its fullness." How to allow that joy to be in us? How do we bask in that joy? How do we in some way let that joy expand from us and touch the lives of many?

John's Gospel says that "He is the light that enlightens every person who comes into the world." How does that happen? Through you! Through me! That light did not just shine two thousand years ago and then go out. It is shining here and now. It is in each of us. Jesus said, "I am the Light of the World." But then He said, "You are the light of the world." Do you experience your own light? — at least a pilot light deep within yourself? Every one of us radiates, not only heat but light. That light in us is intended to shine forth. Light, joy, peace, love.

In my preparation for Advent the thought came to me to reflect upon the gifts that I have been given. I began in my little prayer journal to write out the gifts. What are the most significant gifts that you have received throughout your life? It was a wonderful meditation. Then I meditated on the gifts I have given. My list of gifts received is far greater than the lists of gifts I have given. Then I thought of the joys. What do we have to rejoice in? What are the joys in your life? Can you name your joy? There's no way of being Christian unless you reflect and contemplate and meditate.

The Responsorial Psalm on the Feast of Our Lady of Guadalupe is the Magnificat, Mary's prayer in the first chapter of Luke. Older than the Hail Mary, yet how few of us know that great prayer of Mary: "My soul magnifies the Lord and my spirit dances within me because of all the wonderful things He has done for me." What do you have to rejoice in at this moment? Can you name your joys during this Advent: the joy of being able to get out of bed, the joy of having a car (let alone having it work), the joy of coming to church to find the doors are open, the joy of having a comfortable church, the joy of your own family, the joy that has come to our world over the last decades: the Berlin wall coming down — remember that joy, that impossibility that would never happen in our lifetime, and it happened; the signing of the peace accord between Israel and the Palestinians (let's pray that it will be effective). What are your joys? It's important to recognize that Mary remembered and treasured all these things in her heart. You should stir them up again and again in your own heart.

Recently I visited a couple whom I've known for many years. They are an extraordinary couple. When he was in Viet Nam, he made a promise that if he survived he would give the rest of his life to the Lord in some way, he didn't know how. They had one daughter and the joy she brought them made them aware of how many children never have a home. Together they made a covenant that they would adopt children that no one else wanted. They have adopted five handicapped children.

They had invited me for their twenty-fifth anniversary but I was unable to make it. Instead, I went last week to celebrate dinner with them.

I remember they had came down to St. Agnes Parish the first time my car was stolen and totaled. They had just bought a brand new Pinto, and I told them what had happened to my car. The next day they came back and gave me the keys to their brand new car, just like that. Now that's extraordinary. It's the only car anyone ever gave me.

But there are so many people who deep within themselves have an awesome capacity to love, to be happy.

As we were at dinner, one of their children interrupted about every three minutes, but their common peace in handling that grown up mentally-retarded person was something to behold. I was humbled by their joy and their peace.

I remember another time having dinner with a large family — I think there were eight children — and I had a priest classmate with me. Theresa was the youngest one at that time, she was about four years old. In the middle of the dinner, Keith bent over to her and whispered something in her ear. She just beamed and looked up to him and said, "Tell me again." He had simply said, "I love you." And, four years old, she said, "Tell me again."

Whatever age we are, there's something within us that cries out, "Tell me again." Advent time is our way of trying to celebrate that He is always loving us. We always need to be told again and again because we so easily forget.

What is your level of joy? How do you rejoice? How do you pray always? How are you always thankful? How are you Eucharist? I have a special ministry in terms of trying to rejoice. How do you come to Eucharist? When you come, you are not coming to a wake service. He is not dead.

I think of our faces as a small sacramental. Everyone has many faces. Most often faces are expressionless, if not sad. How does our light get into the world? I think the first step is working on our face. You don't get the blunt of it, those who look at you do. So at least when you come to receive the Body and Blood of Christ, recall that you are not coming to a wake service. Now, it may crack your faces, but try smiling. Turn to the person next to you and see if you can draw a smile from him or her right now. Just practice that. It doesn't hurt, does it? This should be a sign of the light and love in us, to allow ourselves to be stirred up. What if I was really meeting the Lord Jesus? What if He was really coming into me and wanted me to be His light, His joy, His hope, His love for the world? What if I am to be John the Baptist of today in my family?

One of the altar boys told me this morning that his father is an usher today, and he said, "I think I inspired him." What a joy was on his face! How will you let yourself be "inspired" by your children today? How will you inspire your children, draw out of them the joy, the light, the hope that is in them? Pray always. Rejoice in the Lord, again and again. Always be thankful. Be Eucharist. Smile. Jesus really loves you. Tell me again!

Christmas Only Happens in You

How far is it to Bethlehem? How long does it take? Will we get there? It takes 16 hours from Detroit Metropolitan Airport by way of Frankfort and Tel Aviv around Jerusalem into Bethlehem. On Christmas Eve in 1992, I was in Bethlehem. At eight o'clock I celebrated Mass in Shepherd's Field in a grotto that had perhaps been a place where shepherds took shelter. At ten o'clock another priest and I went into the city of Bethlehem. It was raining. The Israeli military had three check points. It took an hour and a half to be checked through security. Once we finally entered the Basilica of the Nativity, there was only standing room.

I was at Tantur for four months at the Ecumenical Institute for Theology in Jerusalem. My room faced the city of Bethlehem. Morning, noon, and night, I looked upon that small little village and wondered what had happened there, and what is still happening.

How long does it take to get to Bethlehem? Will we get there? We are a people of faith. We have come because we believe, not just in something that happened long ago. We believe that there is something new to every Christmas. We easily speak about a "New Year," but far more important is a "New Christmas," is the new birth that each of us is invited to experience. But how long does it take to allow ourselves to believe the incredible, inexhaustible reality that our God has become human?

In the liturgy, three different Masses are assigned to Christmas. At the midnight Mass, the eternal birth of the Son from the Father is celebrated. At the dawn Mass, we celebrate Mary giving birth to Jesus in His humanity. The third Mass of Christmas celebrates the mystical birth of God in us, that mystery that He came not just at a different time and place in ancient history, but that He is always coming to us. The most important crib is not the one that is in church or our home, but it is that crib in our hearts. Unless we really believe that all this wonderful beauty is but a mirror of that which we carry within ourselves, then we do not get to Bethlehem, and Bethlehem does not get to us.

O little town of Bethlehem! O little town of your own home! What is happening tonight? What is happening in us? Are we excited? Do we have any idea how excited the Father, the Son, the Holy Spirit are in terms of the gift they want to give us?

How bleak it was in Bethlehem in 1992! The hatred, the absurdity, the madness of human violence toward one another! I wondered why I was there, but I knew I had to be there. In some way I had to more deeply experience the Truth and the Mystery.

Some are like shepherds who are called at the last moment. None of us is really ready for Christmas, no matter how many Christmases we have experienced. Some, like the wise men, the magi, have been on journey for a long, long time. Some people prepare the day after Christmas for next Christmas.

How do we prepare? How do we allow this mystery to touch us? Do we give ourselves the kind of time necessary? Do we really understand, or do we feel more like the dumb animals who were there but unaware? Jesus has not come into the world in order to become a pious memory. He has come into the world to live in our lives. He has come to give us a new life, a new joy. Each of us should be adorned like a Christmas tree, from head to foot!

We are invited to live in a different way than ever before. We could never get to Bethlehem by ourselves. We could never discover Him by ourselves. So He comes to each of us. Every Christmas contains all our Christmases. Christmas tonight and always is

Eucharist. He comes. He comes. He comes. Not for a moment, but to live in a new way, with a new hope, with a new joy. Who will receive Him? Who will recognize Him? What will happen this week? Will we allow Him to bring something new out of us, a new kind of understanding, a new kind of forgiveness, a new kind of patience, a new kind of joy?

Christmas does not "happen." We happen. We are called to believe, to hope, and to love in a new way.

I saw Mary tonight. At 4:30, just before my exit on the freeway. There was a car accident. Sitting on the embankment, holding her child, rocking back and forth was a black madonna. I had a vision of Mary tonight on I-94.

Each one of us in some way will see and hear and feel something we have never experienced before. Christmas will happen when His presence in us gives us new eyes, a new heart, and we can never be the same again.

Come. Come. Let us adore Him, Christ the Lord.

WHOSE BIRTHDAY IS IT?

December 25, any year: Whose birthday is it? So often we forget What Christmas is all about — at least, the commercial world does. What a marvelous invitation we receive each year to remember whose birthday it is. Christ was born over 2,000 years ago; and Christ continues to gestate in the womb of our hearts. Angelus Silesius, a 17th century mystic and poet, wrote a simple poem that beautifully expresses the meaning of Christmas:

> Christ can be born
> a thousand times in Bethlehem
> but all in vain
> until He is born in me.

In preparation for Christmas, it is good to travel to Bethlehem; not the Bethlehem of Israel, but the Bethlehem within ourselves, within our own hearts.

Jesus is always ready to give us a new birth. Are we ready? How much do we long for Him to touch us in a way that we have never been touched before?

The early Christians cried out, "Maranatha" — "Come, Lord Jesus, Come." That certainly is our prayer. We want the Lord to come more and more deeply in us, more than ever before in our lives. The world is filled with so many new and promising things. There are meetings all over the world between nations who have been as strangers to us, promises of hope that there might be peace in the land where Our Lord was born. We know Christ as the Prince of Peace, and yet, after 2,000 years, so much violence continues. Still, Christ's love and peace born and lived out in us is a promise — hope in a world crying out for new birth.

How well we know the joyful mystery of the Visitation; how often we have meditated on it. Mary was told that she was to be the mother of God. The first word of the new covenant was the word "rejoice." "Rejoice, Mary, the Lord is with you." We want to celebrate that great news again and again! We never celebrate it enough. And again, I say REJOICE!

What was said to Mary is said to all of us. Mary accomplished her mission. We are still in the process of living out our mission. So, to each one of us, the angel is saying, "Rejoice, the Lord is with you." Every liturgy proclaims that message and enables us to experience it more totally in our lives. The Lord is with you. The Lord is with us. Mary received that incredible Word and she said her "yes." Then, she was told about her cousin, Elizabeth, who though beyond the age of childbearing had already conceived and was in the sixth month of her pregnancy. The angel did not tell Mary to go and visit Elizabeth. The angel simply said, "Your cousin, Elizabeth, is with child and she is now in her sixth month."

What did Mary do? Immediately, or perhaps a better translation, "with full awareness," "deliberately," she went to help her cousin. How many people do we know about who are in need of help? No one sends us. We simply know about it. How important it is to open our eyes and ears to find out who needs us. There are 5,000 homeless people in the city of Detroit at any given time. Yet that, perhaps, is not the worse kind of suffering. Mother Theresa said that the most painful kind of suffering is aloneness, of being unloved, of being unknown. Probably, even within our own family, there are those with whom we have not talked in a long time. How many are in our neighborhood whose names we do not know?

Christmas is the birth of the Good News. Rejoice, the Lord is with you.

Mary went in haste to visit her cousin, Elizabeth. As soon as Elizabeth saw Mary, John in her womb leaped for joy. Elizabeth recognized what this meant and cried out, "How is it that the mother of my Lord should come to me?" Then Elizabeth uttered the beautiful prayer: "Hail Mary... Rejoice Mary. Blessed are you among women and blessed is the fruit of your womb," Jesus. These words of praise and joy spoken over 2,000 years ago are meant for us to share with one another today. How astonished we would be if someone would come to us in the faith of those words! What a grace it is in us to be able to recognize the hidden presence of Christ in others! Will we ever get over the wonder of it? Will we ever dare to acknowledge the people of faith in our lives and cry out as Elizabeth did, "Blessed are you... Blessed are you who come to me... Blessed are you who share this faith."

The most extraordinary thing about Mary is that she is so ordinary. Mary never performed a miracle, she never spoke to the crowd. Mary: All she did was to say "Yes." All she did was to go to her cousin to be a servant, to be of help to her, to be Mary. That was her mission. That is our mission. We are not called to be extraordinary. Our mission will never get into the newspapers. All we are asked to say is "Yes" to the Word of God — and, to be aware of the people in our lives, to forget ourselves for a little while and give others some of our time, some of our joy, simply our presence. This was the mission of Mary, this is the mission of each of us.

What a wonderful and sensitive awareness Mary must have had of other people! At that great miracle of Cana, Mary simply observed that they had no wine. She said to Jesus, "They have no wine." She did not make a big to-do about it; she simply was aware that they did not have enough wine. Then she directed the servants, "Do whatever He tells you." And she had credentials to do that, because she heard the Word of God and lived it.

What will make Christmas for us? How long will it take to allow Jesus to come, to find a place in us? How many people are already knocking and asking if there is room in the inn of our hearts? Is there room? Is there time for Jesus this year in us?

Christmas! There is no date on the calendar we are more aware of. There is no more lavish preparation on the part of the whole world. Will we take the time to try to understand and to respond to what has happened? Will we recognize what is always going on, things of which we are so rarely aware? Do we dare to abandon ourselves to the love of Abba, who is always loving us into existence. At every moment, Abba is giving us Jesus. He did not do it just once upon a time. At every moment, Abba is giving us Jesus. We are invited to say our "Yes" to the love of Abba.

Our second "Yes," our second act of abandonment, is to the Eucharist. Christmas comes every day, because Jesus gives Himself to us under the form of bread and wine — not just for ourselves, but for all those He gives to us. He intends us to become gift, gift to the world. The whole world is embraced with the Eucharist each day. Will we say our "Yes"? Will we abandon ourselves to the Eucharist, so that we can become like Mary? She said her "Yes" and immediately she became servant. The sign that we are Eucharistic is that we no longer live for ourselves. We become available for others.

And the third "Yes," the third act of abandonment, is to the presence of the Holy Spirit in each one of us — even the most unlikely of us. What a tremendous act of faith and hope and love we are drawn to each day! What a tremendous level of love to be present, to recognize the love of Abba for us, to open ourselves to the gift of the Eucharist, to say our "Yes, here I am." With that we recognize that the Lord's presence is never ended, it is always just begun. We begin all over again to say our "Yes" to one another, to all those whom we have been forgetting, to say our "Yes, Yes, Yes" and to allow Jesus to do something wonderful in us. We could well pray until it becomes almost a part of our breathing — "Rejoice Mary... rejoice John... rejoice Angela... rejoice Howard... the Lord is with you. Blessed are you among women and men, blessed are you to be in this city, blessed are you who are unknown and un-understood, blessed are you because that is the way it was with Christ Jesus. So it always will be for those who believe and hope and love."

The Lord is with you. Who are we that the love of our Lord should come to us? Who are we that Christ should come to us again and again? Jesus comes to us so that we can become gift. We are always being sent forth to be gift, to be sacrament, to be joy and hope. As Christians, this is who we are, who we are becoming. Let us lift up our hearts, let us take the time to say our "Yes," let us take our time each day to become gift. Let us dare to believe that Christ is taking our bodies to be gift to others. Let us dare to believe that we are Christ's presence sent forth. We have cause to celebrate. We rejoice for all Christ has done, for all that Christ continues to do for us, in us, and through us.

Whose birthday is it anyway? Happy birthday to Jesus. Happy birthday to all who recognize the Lord born anew in their hearts as gift to the world. Rejoice, the Lord is with you. Yes, blessed are all who know that the promise of Christ to live in the womb of their heart is being fulfilled in them today!

For Us

Come ye — Come you to Bethlehem. We sang this song as children. I never thought that some day I would be able to respond to that hymn, but at Christmas in 1992 I was in Bethlehem. I had carried with me the print-out of the parishioners' names. It weighed a pound and a half. I prayed the name of every member of the parish — of all 1400 families — at Midnight Mass in Bethlehem. In some way I deposited at least their names in that holy place.

Come. Come ye to Bethlehem. Come let us adore Him. How do we do that? We sing hymns too easily. How do we adore Him this morning? How do we name that experience?

I was in Shepherd Field for the Midnight Mass, then in the Basilica for the noon Mass. I felt simply "held" there. I was trying to understand what this moment was. For four months I could look out my window and see Bethlehem — morning, noon, and night. I tried in some way to reflect and to ponder it and treasure it in my heart so I would never forget it — so that it would never leave me.

How do we understand Christmas, this moment? What is new? If we could only *name* our experience!

Some people get a new ornament for their tree each year. Some people get a new crib each year. Some people get a sculpture. Why do we bring a tree into our house? Why do we decorate our homes and yards? What is it that we are attempting, in some way, to experience? Even those who have no faith light up their homes, give gifts. There is something mysterious about this moment that, even after 2000 years, continues to fall upon us.

Do you remember being in Bethlehem a thousand years ago? Something of us was around two thousand years ago. Each of us is carrying thousands of years of the genetic code. Something of us was there, but it seems too much to grasp.

How do you name your Christmas year? How do we name what has happened to us? What happened in those shepherds as they were drawn to Bethlehem? They were astonished at what was said to them. Imagine how much more astonished were those to whom they gave their message. It is almost absurd to think that God, the Creator of the galaxy, of this universe that is so immense, could come to be with us — not as an all-powerful God bringing terror and fear, but as a loving God who became an infant, a little child of whom no one would be afraid. Who are we that God could become conscious of us? What we're trying to understand is that everything has changed. Each one of us is infinitely significant.

As I read those 1400 names in Bethlehem that Christmas, I often didn't have a clue as to the people, the faces, the families represented by those names. Most were anonymous names to me, but I prayed them. How few faces I can name! Yet, every one of us has a name, and we have a history, and we are infinitely important.

Few ever go to Bethlehem, so Bethlehem comes to us. Christmas is but a mirror of who you are and what you are coming to be. There is in each of us an immense dream, a desire, a hope for something more. God is that something more. His presence in us is not a myth. It's not a symbol. It is a fact. It may seem absurd, impossible — but our God is so immense that He asks of us an almost impossible faith. Only God, our God who made us, could dream of coming to be *in* us. If only we could hold onto this. If only Christmas could be every day. We do not have the capacity to sustain such an excitement, such astonishment, but we do pray each day, "Give us this day our daily bread. Give us this day our daily Christmas." He comes, not only today, but He's always coming to us. There is a reality to our deepest hunger, our deepest longing.

What is your word for Christmas? The awesomeness, the wonder, the incredibility.... How do you name the ring of the tree of your Christmas life each year? I think the most important words for me are "*for us*." To think that the Word, that the Eternal Consciousness, that Love, has become human *for us* — for you and for me.... No matter where we have been, no matter how much we have forgotten, no matter how much we have denied, He still comes to us. This God of ours is too much, too incredible, so beyond our capacity to comprehend. But He has come. For us. This is not a myth. This is not a symbol. It is a fact. He is real, regardless of our own poverty in trying to understand.

Again and again we come to Bethlehem and we carry within us all the generations that have brought us to this moment. "The hopes and dreams of all the years are met in us this day." The almighty Word, in the midst of the night, leapt down from heaven and has come to us. If we could only believe. If we could only let the little child leap for joy in us, we couldn't leave. We'd be compelled to stay here, to linger, because there is nothing more important in the whole of our life than the faith He has given us to believe, to bow down, to adore, to reflect, to cherish, to treasure, to dare to believe that He has come for you and for me. Not for a moment. But every day.

Every liturgy we hear again, "This is My Body given for you. This is My Blood to be shed for you." How hidden! How impossible! When He was born, no one knew it for thirty years except Mary, Joseph, those few shepherds... and it's not much different today. How many recognize who He is? What has come to us is so hidden, yet each of you are the shepherds of old, the magi of old. You cannot *not* believe. What an immense gift that is given to us. "And Mary reflected, cherished, pondered all these things in her heart all the days of her life." We are intended each day to pause in that mystery of our daily bread of Christmas.

Come. Come you to Bethlehem. Come let us adore. Let us allow ourselves to be loved. Let ourselves be freed from all our fears and our anxieties. We belong to a Savior who knows us by name and comes to give us the gift that is the source of all gifts. Come. Let us adore.

Do You See What I See?

What a fascinating and intriguing narrative is the story of the three kings. We can understand the shepherds being drawn by the angel to Bethlehem, but now we hear this mysterious story about magi, of astrologers or astronomers, led not by angels but by a phenomenon of nature. They were led by a star to Bethlehem. Who were these people? Where did they come from? What happened to them afterwards?

You may have heard the story of the fourth magi, the one who lost his way and didn't find Jesus until he found him at the foot of the cross. We don't know how many magi there were, we claim three because of the three gifts. But what is important is to recognize that this happened not just long ago, but that it is continuing to happen this day. Jesus is the light that enlightens everyone who comes into the world. So today is your feast. Who are these magi today? How does this story touch your life? How does it involve you? Because every passage of Scripture is a mirror that tells us something about ourselves — it is not just a moment of history of long ago. It is today. How does this story touch you? How does it reveal a facet of your life that perhaps you rarely reflect upon? We are all called to enter that prayerful attitude of Mary who reflected and pondered and meditated these things in her heart. What happened in those magi, those astronomers, those studiers of stars?

Everyone of us at one time or another has been fascinated and intrigued by the night sky. Today, as never before, we know something of what lies out there. Perhaps our astronomers are our magi of today — who most readily kneel before the mystery of the infinity of the universe. Never before have we known so much and been so awed by the universe. All of us could well study some of the galaxies, could touch something of the mystery of our own life, of who we are and who we are called to become. What happened to these men or women who saw a star and left everything to follow it? Not just for a day or an hour, but upwards of two years they were on this mysterious journey. Perhaps they did not start out together. Perhaps they came from different continents. Bethlehem stands in the center where Europe and Asia and Africa come together. Were they from Asia? Were they from Africa? Were they from Europe? Or did they somehow converge, join together — and what a joy it must have been when they found someone else who was as mad and as foolish as they were.

Imagine following a star. If you were to see a star tonight that in some way touched you very deeply, can you imagine letting go everything to follow that star? If your family could catch up with you, they'd put you in a psychiatric unit! Those things are not done. But there are mysterious moments in our life, when we become very foolish.

What's the most foolish thing you ever did in your life? — aside from getting married, or becoming a religious, or becoming a priest?

That mystery! There is a light in every one of us, and all of you have responded to that light. There's a searching in each of us. There's a hunger. Every once in a while we drop into that mystery within. We are supposed to reflect, to meditate, to ponder on the significance of the events of our existence. Our life is so full of mystery that we run away from them most of the time. We are invited to reflect, to discover that something of the magi in each of us. There's something very foolish in us. There's something in us that can forget our self, that desires to follow the star, that yearns for the light wherever it leads.

What must have been in those men and women of long ago and what is in the hearts of men and women of today to let go of all things to follow the beckoning, the invitation. Have you been faithful to the light that has been passed down from your parents? Do you carry it ablaze within you? So many no longer carry the light. They've been "extinguished." The light has to be lit again and again and again. How in your life have you been faithful to that light, and again and again enkindled it? How, in your adult life, were you drawn to the mystery of Christ? How many of you made a decision as adults to become a member of our faith community? Again and again through the years we have made decisions to be faithful, to follow the light. That light is always coming into the world.

What was the light of that star? It was the Holy Trinity: Father, Son, and Holy Spirit. Because all things have come from The Three: Father, Son, and Holy Spirit. So the star and the magi were lit by something beyond themselves. Few of us would have the courage to follow the light, to leave our country, to leave everything.

The mystery we celebrate is not that we have followed the star, that we've discovered the light, but that the Father, Son, and Holy Spirit are the magi. *They* have found *us* regardless where we have been, where we have wandered. Each one of us is a witness that Father, Son, and Holy Spirit have come to us and given us the gifts of our faith, our hope, and our love. How many times that light might have become very dim, but somehow we were faithful to that light! This mystery, unknown to the rest of the world, made known to us! It is light coming to us.

We respond to the light in bringing our gifts to Him. What are your gifts this year? What Christmas gift did you bring to the crib? What is the gold of your life? What is the frankincense? What is the myrrh?

Perhaps the gold is simply your ordinary day. Most of us lead very ordinary lives. We live, we love, we suffer, we grow. Just the faithfulness to being father and mother, to being son and daughter, to being friend and family. This is the gold of everyday. The frankincense may be our prayer, our meditation, our reflection, our dream, our hoping: that which gives meaning to our life, that which brings us joy. The myrrh is the symbol of suffering that is unavoidable, that is part of the redemptive mystery: Jesus did not take away suffering, but He promised He'd be with us through it all.

The Feast of the Epiphany is never over. The light that enlightens each of us is still shining. It comes to us in a new way day by day. He's always drawing us closer. Always drawing us deeper. What is the star of your life? What do you allow to lead you? Do you recognize who it is that comes to you, that kneels before you?

Imagine the immense energy, the immense journey of God becoming human in order to be in our life. He comes to us in a special way each time we receive the Body and Blood of Christ. He comes that we can become the light and life of the world. He has no one else today except us. So today is our feast day. We are the magi. We are the ones who follow the star. We are the ones who recognize the light. We are the ones He comes to, that we might be the light and the life of the whole world. Let us continue to be drawn, to adore Him, and to recognize the mystery that is His life in us.

AND NOW WE BEGIN

Jesus went to the Jordan and was baptized by John. How extraordinary! Jesus was baptized by John! The Son of God baptized by water! As Jesus left Nazareth and went down to the Jordan River, He could have continued south to Jerusalem.

I wonder, as Jesus was growing up, did He ever think about what He would like to be? At twelve years old, He was in the Temple teaching the doctors, the learned ones. Did He ever think about becoming a rabbi, a teacher, a priest? What went on in His young mind?

He could have gone south to Jerusalem to become a professor, a professional person, a "big name." But Jesus didn't go south to Jerusalem; He turned to the left and went to the Jordan where the ordinary people, by the thousands, came out to be baptized by a wild man of the desert. There Jesus stood in line and was baptized. When He was baptized, the heavens opened up and a dove descended upon Him, the Holy Spirit, and a voice was heard: "This is My beloved Son on Whom My favor rests."

Only three times in all of the New Testament do we hear the voice of the Father, and it's always the same words: "This is My beloved. Listen."

Are you ready for baptism? Would you go to the Jordan River to be baptized today by this wild man of the desert? Aren't you glad your parents baptized you before you became aware of what was happening to you? Most of us probably wouldn't have found our way. We feel gratitude for the heritage of our faith and that we were baptized early. But that is never enough: the baptism by water. Have you been baptized yet by fire? by the Holy Spirit?

Is your baptism still alive in you or is it a certificate long forgotten? Can you still taste your baptism? Does it sometimes flame up? Do you recognize that your baptism is not something past, but is alive and something to be lived into? It's not over; it's hardly begun. You have been scorched and singed by the Holy Spirit, not by water.

Recently I visited a family, a broken home. The son had finally got away from his father who was very abusive. I asked him if he would like to be baptized. He was twelve years old, too. And he said, "What is it to be baptized?" I said, "Well, you know about Jesus...." He said, "Jesus? Oh, He's the one they put nails into." I found I was inarticulate; I didn't know how to describe to this twelve-year-old what it would be to be baptized. What would it be to come into a new family? What is it to be baptized?

To be baptized is to be plunged into the Father, Son, and Holy Spirit. To find a new family. To know that you will never be alone again. To be given a new identity. To experience a new call. To know the Father. To live in the Son. To be inflamed by the Holy Spirit. How can you explain this to a child? But in some way, something happened. As I was leaving he asked, "Can I change my name?" A twelve-year-old who wants to change his name, to find a new identity, to find a new family, understands baptism.

Recently we had perhaps the most spectacular liturgy in the diocese that I've seen in all my life. Two men, close friends of mine, became bishops. The music was wonderful. The trumpets were perfectly in tune. There was standing room only. I've never seen the Cathedral more luxurious with flowers. Everyone was lifted up.

I wish that we could celebrate our baptism — each one of us — in this way. Those men, becoming bishops, were simply living into their baptism. Their most significant moment was not this recent celebration; it was the day they were baptized, where they were drawn into Christ, and where Christ came into them. Being a bishop is just a facet. The most important call is not to be bishop or priest or religious or even pope; our identity, who we are, comes in baptism. Most important is that we are called to be holy, that we are called to be one with God, that we are wanted by God, that we are loved by God.

We have, each of us, an immense mission and work in life. We are not anonymous. Each one of us is wonderfully and terribly significant. The Father, Son, and Holy Spirit know us, and claim us. There is never a moment that the Father is not thinking about us and loving us and calling us into a more abundant life. How often we pray to Him, "Give us today our daily bread." Today. Our Christian faith is not a past or a future; it's always a now. This day. Our daily bread. Give us today our daily Christmas. Give us today a new consciousness that our baptism is a well that springs up into life everlasting. How little of our life have we really lived! How little of our grace have we recognized! How little of our baptism have we really tasted! We have been anointed. The Holy Spirit has descended upon us. We carry something within us that is capable of going to the ends of the earth. Jesus said, "Go you to all nations, to the end of the world, baptizing," — including your family, the whole world. So we have barely begun.

Our baptism is not over and done with. The outer excitement is fading away, but something did happen. We were given new life, and we are given it every day of our lives. We come to each liturgy to renew our baptism, our identity, and our consciousness of what it is to be "in Christ," to carry that name. We come to be renewed and to have the grace stirred within us. But this is the launching pad. This is not the terminal. We are being sent forth, to be a light, to be a hope, and to be a joy. To make a difference.

Have you been baptized? Does Jesus make a difference in your life? Are you distinctive? Does an aura, a radiation, extend out from you to others? We are called again to go to the Jordan, to be baptized again, not by water, but to recognize that today, every day of our lives, the heavens open and the Holy Spirit descends upon us. We are invited to hear and to experience what Jesus heard and experienced: "You are my beloved daughter. You are my beloved son. My favor, my grace, my love rest upon you. Go and give your baptism to the whole world."

Post Script: Thoughts on the Millennium

A Conversation with Father Ed Farrell

What is the significance of the millennium for Christians?

The millennium is a time of special grace. It is a time for conversion, a time for gratitude. It is an opportunity to praise God, to thank God for all that has been and for all that is yet to come.

It is hard for any generation to look back or look forward. I have asked many people what their thoughts are about the new millennium. I have not found one person who really has many expectations of the next hundred years, let alone 500 or 1,000 years. Part of that is because people are so involved and absorbed in the day-to-day. There is not that opportunity to envision the future.

What are your expectations for the next millennium?

Christians are people of hope. We believe in a God who, as Revelation 21 says, is "making all things new." This new creation is unfolding. In spite of the many atrocities of the past century, I see more signs of hope than of despair. Never before have we had the economical resources to end poverty throughout all the world. We are seeing compassion as never before. The past century has seen a number of moral revolutions, including the recognition of sexism and racism, even though we are still segregated in so many ways.

There is a growing global unity in terms of economics and in terms of culture. There is exchange and affirmation and appreciation as never before in history. There is also a growing appreciation of the gifts of others in terms of religion. In this new millennium, I predict there will be a new understanding of the major world religions as well as unity between denominations.

Out of these developments, there will be a new concentration on human development. I hope people will be able to continue their education, not just academically, but in terms of the truth of being who they are, being able to develop themselves and their relationships fully. People do not know how to relate, because of their backgrounds and because so many are wounded. The Church will be involved in a much more radical way with the healing of people. As people live longer, there will be an increasing number who are able to volunteer and see their lives in terms of human services rather than just economic goals. This will allow the Church to become more involved in special ministries with youth, in cities, and in prisons.

That's quite a lot of hopeful vision for the future. What on the horizon worries or concerns you?

Teilhard de Chardin was very hopeful, but he also had a dread that we would devolve rather than evolve. These hopes are not going to come just because of wishful thinking. Never before have we needed more dedicated leaders in the realm of politics, education, social services, and religion. Never before have we needed Christianity more. The vision of the Gospel is a vision of hope. It's not optimism. It's not Pollyanna, but it takes immense work and dedication. It might even take lowering our standard of living — to live more simply, as someone said, that others may simply live.

In the decades immediately ahead of us, we have immense problems to address: What are we going to do with our cities? with all the issues facing our youth? with our prisons? One could get very cynical, especially when one recognizes the power of evil in the human heart and institutions. I believe the twenty-first century is going to set the pattern for the next nine centuries. It depends on our choice. Although the Church may be shrinking percentage wise in terms of the overall population of the globe, as Christians we must deepen our faith and become very decisive in terms of our ministry. The Church is a launching base to enter into the heart of the world, to be the witnesses and to carry out that revolution that has only barely begun.

Does this event of the year 2000 give us any insight into the Second Coming or Christ's return?

Christ came first without our asking, and I believe he will come again when we will have lived out the Gospel and actualized the Good News. The dream of world unity and peace has been a dream of all times, but the tools have not been there. In our time we have the technological tools, but the revolution has to be in the human heart. Christianity must help people discover the indwelling presence of God and to reverence the mystery in the other person. So much has to be unlearned.

The more we recognize Christ's presence in ourselves, the greater capacity we have to recognize it in others. Christ has overcome the world and all our violence. He has taken it on himself. We have everything we need to create a civilization of love. How long will it take?

How are Christians called to respond to this time of transition?

The first message of John the Baptist was: "Repent, for the kingdom of heaven is at hand." At the millennium, there needs to be a radical repentance for what we've done to one another. John Perkins has coined the three R's: relocation, redistribution, reconciliation. We have to relocate our minds and our hearts. We have to redistribute that which we have taken from others and which belongs to others. Then and only then can we have reconciliation. John Paul II said that one of the sadnesses of our time is that so many people have lost the capacity to experience the joy of reconciliation, the joy of forgiveness. There is real sin in the world, and it cannot be explained away by psychology. People need to recognize their sin, and they need to repent. If you don't pray, then you don't even recognize your sin. It is a call to pray so that we can see who we are and recognize who we are called to become. If we do not, then nothing is going to change.

There is a new vision that holiness is not just for extraordinary people, but that ordinary people are called to be holy. Christ brought a new phenomenon, a new capacity to the human person. The Incarnation was the greatest thing that happened since Creation, and it was greater than Creation. He has broken into our lives, and now everyone has the capacity to be like Christ. The problem is for people to believe in the gifts they already have. Many people have a negative self-image, and they act out of that, and it determines the direction of their lives. We need to hear the Good News.

Even though our sin is like scarlet, God forgives us seventy times seven. That's a lot of forgiveness. When we receive that forgiveness, we can offer compassion and forgive others for not living up to our expectations. As the psalmist said, we need new eyes, new ears. We need a new heart. We need a heart transplant. The Church is the medium of doing that.

In what ways do you see the Holy Spirit brooding over the world?

Down through the ages there have been many speaking about the "Third Age," that of the Holy Spirit. I think the discovery of the Holy Spirit is going to be part of the unfolding of this millennium. A new outpouring of the Holy Spirit started at the turn of the last century with the beginning of the ecumenical, Pentecostal, and the charismatic movements. The great teaching of the third millennium is to discover the Trinity and the call for us to have a personal relationship to each Person of the Trinity.

The work of the Holy Spirit is reconciliation, community, forgiveness, healing, and peace. If we don't have union with God, we can't be in communion with one another. If we do not have peace within ourselves, we create violence. The discovery that the inner being is filled with peace, joy, and healing — that is going to be the great metanoia. This will allow us to bring philosophy, science, technology, and politics into a new kind of unity of service, which will be marked by compassion, collaboration, and cooperation. We should not settle for "what we have now is as good as it gets." It can be a lot better!

This book was designed and published by St. Pauls/
Alba House, the publishing arm of the Society of St.
Paul, an international religious congregation of priests
and brothers dedicated to serving the Church through
the communications media. For information regarding
this and associated ministries of the Pauline Family of
Congregations, write to the Vocation Director, Society
of St. Paul, 7050 Pinehurst, Dearborn, Michigan 48126
or check our internet site, www.albahouse.org